Teresa Hayter

The Creation of World Poverty

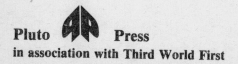

Pluto Press

in association with Third World First

This edition first published by Pluto Press Limited,
Unit 10 Spencer Court, 7 Chalcot Road, London NW1 8LH

Copyright © Teresa Hayter and Third World First 1981

ISBN 0 86104 339 1

Cover drawing by Chris Madden
Cover design by Clive Challis
Typeset by Grassroots Typeset, London. (tel: 01-328 0318)
Printed in Great Britain by Photobooks (Bristol) Limited,
28 Midland Road, Bristol.

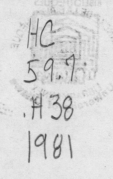

Contents

In 1517, the Spanish missionary Bartolomé de las Casas, taking great pity on the Indians who were languishing in the hellish workpits of Antillean gold mines, suggested to Charles V, king of Spain, a scheme of importing blacks, so that they might languish in the hellish workpits of Antillean gold mines. To this odd philanthropic twist we owe... endless things... (Jorge Luis Borge, *A Universal History of Infamy*)

Foreword

I want to thank Third World First very much for suggesting that I write this book and for efficiently obtaining funding to enable me to write it. I also want particularly to thank the following people for their comments and advice: Hilary Scannell and Ian Campbell of Third World First; the editors of Pluto Press; and André Gunder Frank, Keith Griffin, Bob Sutcliffe and Gavin Williams, whose ideas and writings I have pillaged, with their consent I hope. None of them is of course responsible for anything I have written, and I probably haven't made as much use of their advice as I should have.

I have not cluttered up the text with references to all the material I have drawn on. There is a bibliography which lists the books, articles and sources I have used most extensively and a further guide to reading will be found in Third World First's annotated book list, *Books against Poverty*, Third World First 1980.

Teresa Hayter

6

Introduction

by Third World First

On the cover of the 1980 Brandt Report* a snaky black line wriggles across a world map, marking off the wealth divide between 'North' and 'South'

'Northern' people often suffer a double shock when they first peer across that line. There is the shock of glimpsing what poverty and oppression mean for 800 million human beings. And there is the shock of hearing the radical *explanations* of that poverty, which are not only disturbing, but often seem like a bolt from the blue.

Yet the radical analysis is not new. If it seems startling, that is probably because in 'northern' societies like Britain it is very rarely heard. It has to battle for a hearing against a tranquillising consensus that drips constantly from TV, radio, newspapers, school textbooks and charity advertisements.

The consensus takes it for granted that the Third World has always been poor, and that development comes from the 'north' to save the 'south', beginning with the industrial revolution and maturing with the microchip. When challenged by history, it shuffles sideways, lifts its eyebrows, and adopts a superior tone: 'Focusing on questions of historical guilt will not provide answers... Self-righteousness will neither create jobs nor feed hungry mouths.' (Brandt Report, p.25).

But suppose the guilty party is not guilty, but out on bail doing the same nefarious deeds as in past history, all in the name of enlightenment, growth, and development? Then it would be useful indeed — and in no way self-righteous — to try to understand this past history, this present behaviour, and the reason for this tragic self-delusion.

Third World First asked the author to write this book in order to help such an understanding. In our education and campaigning work on world development, we know that guilt and self-righteousness are a hindrance, while undirected com-

---

* *North-South: a Programme for Survival*, The Report of the Independent Commission on International Development Issues under the Chairmanship of Willy Brandt, Pan Books 1980, £1.95.

passion will almost inevitably be misdirected. It is vitally important to understand what the radical explanation is, some of the wealth of evidence which supports it, and why it is so consistently ignored, dismissed, or caricatured in British society. Only then is it possible to ask *intelligently* the continuing question, 'what should we do?'

The aim of *The Creation of World Poverty* is quite modest. If it convinces you that the radical analysis of Third World poverty is neither an irrelevant bit of history nor a fiendish left-wing plot, but a coherent explanation, backed by solid evidence, which affects thought and action now and is impossible to ignore, then it will have gone a long way towards success.

Third World First is a national movement in British colleges and universities (head office, 232 Cowley Road, Oxford), with a rapidly growing student membership and an expanding programme of education and campaigning on third world issues. Third World First aims:

- to publicise the facts of international poverty;
- to support the poor and oppressed as they organise together to combat poverty and determine their own path of development;
- to expose, and oppose, the interests of the rich and powerful who stand in their way.

Survival

There is these days much talk of 'survival'. The human species appears to be in unprecedented danger, the scene set for nuclear holocaust. In addition, and no less seriously, over half-a-billion people, most of them living in Asia, Africa and Latin America, are threatened with, if not death, at least a life of semi-starvation. The authorities in the industrialised countries of the West are beginning to link this latter phenomenon with their own survival: hence the publication of the Brandt Commission's Report, *North-South: A Programme for Survival*. Unlike the international reports which have preceded it, this one has attracted some continuing attention, much of it uncritical. The book has sold nearly a hundred thousand copies in 1980 in Britain alone.

The concern in the West with extreme poverty in under-developed countries has been intermittent at best. Many of those who support the proposals of the Brandt Report, especially for more 'aid', do so out of genuine humanitarian concern about such poverty. But it is doubtful whether this is the main concern of its authors, and it is certainly not their only concern. The Brandt Commission Report represents currently the most enlightened expression of establishment thinking about international economic matters, and, in particular, about the provision of so-called 'aid' to developing countries. But it would be a mistake to think of its authors as primarily or exclusively concerned with the alleviation of poverty in those countries. They are, instead, *primarily concerned with the preservation of the existing world economic order*. There are nevertheless two important differences between the current and previous states of establishment opinion: first, extreme poverty in underdeveloped countries is now seen as a real threat to the survival of the system rather than as something to be dealt with by occasional philanthropic gestures; and, second, a response is required to the current crisis in the world economy.

The reasons for the first change are not hard to find. In practically every country in the world, there are forces rebelling against the empty promises of political independence, demanding genuine independence and real economic progress, increasingly aware that, just as they were robbed in the past by their colonial rulers, so now they are being robbed by an alliance between these old colonial rulers, some new neo-colonial ones and their own ruling classes. These rebellions have led to quite fundamental changes in social organisation in some parts of the world and to the closing of some countries to profitable private investment.

The problem of containing the disaffection of the poor through military means has been shown most clearly by the failure of the United States war in Vietnam. The use of military force has certainly not been abandoned. Although this can usually be left to local armed forces, as was the case in Chile, these forces are massively armed and assisted by the West. Moreover the United States has threatened the use of nuclear weapons in order to preserve its supplies of oil and the British, in Ireland, are still in the business of using their army to suppress rebellion.

Reforms, in the sense of some alleviation of the harshness of the economic system, could be another way of stabilising this system and it is precisely this that the Brandt Commission Report is proposing: 'all the lessons of reform within national societies confirm the gains for all in a process of change that makes the world a less unequal and a more just and habitable place.' The Report's pleas for 'a world based less on power and status, more on justice and contract' have a genuine ring: 'the idea of a community of nations,' it says, 'has little meaning ... if hunger is regarded as a marginal problem which humanity can live with.' But the members of the Brandt Commission were all, with the semi-exception of Dragoslav Avramovic, nationals of capitalist countries and, many of them, notable beneficiaries of the capitalist system. They argue for a world without ideology; they never openly state that the measures they propose are not to be socialist measures and they even compare achievements in China with failures in India. Yet, although their assumptions are not explicitly stated, it becomes clear from the odd phrase that they are not proposing socialism, or the public ownership of the means of production.

It is clear enough that their implicit model is the 'mixed economy' of social democracy, for instance when they say that 'the satisfaction of the essential needs of the poor requires a combination of private and public goods and services'. They are not interested in solutions that are incompatible with the private ownership of the means of production, however necessary and inevitable such solutions may be. Edward Heath, member of the Brandt Commission, in giving his reasons in an article in the London *Times* for supporting the Brandt proposals, makes this perfectly clear:

> These [least developed] countries may not be of great economic importance to the West. But they are often of vital strategic importance to it. This is true, for example, of Somalia, Bangladesh and Sudan. Like so many other least developed countries in Africa and Asia, their stability is threatened by radical forces whose success is nurtured by economic deprivation and inequality. If these radical forces are given the opportunity to make progress, others like them around the world will also be encouraged. Moderate leaders will conclude that they cannot rely on the West to support them.

The domino theory is not dead. As a lecturer at the United States Army School of the Americas put it:

> Democracy [sic] and communism are engaged in a struggle for objectives of worldwide significance ... The maintenance of military bases and the network of alliances that surround the communist world is not enough to stop the revolutionary war, and, unfortunately, its field of battle is widening every day. Economic aid, another form of subtle penetration, is a particular phase of this struggle, in that the major powers try to obtain dominant influence over developing nations.

The shift in international orthodoxy is to be found not only in the Brandt Report. It is embodied in numerous reports from the United Nations and other international agencies, especially World Bank publications and the International Labour Organisation's publications on 'basic needs', and books such as the World Bank-sponsored *Redistribution with Growth*, *Assault on World Poverty*, and so on. These criticise the failure of past aid policies to achieve any reduction of poverty in the Third World and argue for greater attention to the needs of the very poor. This process is perhaps best symbolised in the person of Mr Robert McNamara, who commissioned the Brandt Report. In the 1960s, as United States Secretary of Defence, he was officially in charge of the bombing of North Vietnam. Then from 1968 to 1981, he was president of the major international 'aid' agency, the World Bank, and presided over a switch in its lending policies towards making more funds available for agriculture, education and, supposedly at least, attention to the basic needs of the very poor whose problems were eloquently expounded in his speeches.

The context for this concern is the world recession. By the end of the seventies, the Brandt Report says, 'the world economy was in serious difficulties, and the institutional framework which had served it since the war was inadequate to resolve them'. In other words the system set up at Bretton Woods after the second world war, at which the International Monetary Fund and the World Bank were established, is crumbling. As the Brandt Report rightly says, we live in a precariously interdependent world. But it maintains that there is hope, if right-minded policies are adopted.

Humanitarian objectives coincide happily, for the Brandt Report, with what are considered to be the 'mutual interests' of the developed and developing countries in expanded markets and expanding fields for investment. This is reminiscent of Joseph Chamberlain, in late nineteenth-century Britain, who argued for the expansion of Empire to develop the 'under-developed estates' of the tropics to the mutual benefit of the peoples of Britain and its colonies. As Heath in *The Times* again says:

> The world food situation is serious, with indications of declining per capita production and record numbers of malnourished people ... This situation affects the industrialised countries in at least two ways. First, it tends to push up world food prices ... Second, chronic malnutrition ... inevitably leads to an inefficient use of resources, persistently low productivity and thus low purchasing power. An improvement in nutritional standards could therefore contribute greatly to an upturn in world economic activity as well as being a moral imperative in its own right.

Thus rather oddly, at a time when governments around the world have discovered the unworkability of the Keynesian model for internal purposes, the Brandt Report proposes a kind of international Keynesianism: the industrialised countries should transfer funds to developing countries to 'prime the pump' by increasing their ability to import from the industrialised countries.

The Brandt Report is strongly opposed to trade protection, including protection against exports from underdeveloped countries to developed countries. Thus it says:

> It is often forgotten that North-South trade is a two-way street. Unless the South exports to the North, it cannot in turn pay for the North's exports to the South. Today the industrialised countries have a large positive balance of trade in manufactures with developing countries. The dependence of the industrialised countries on the markets of the South is substantial and is becoming larger still.

Elsewhere, the Report says:

> That the South needs the North is evident [is it?]. But what of the North's need for the South? In what sense can the South be said to be 'an engine for growth' for the North? It is now acknowledged that in the post-1974 period when the capital surplus oil exporters placed large funds in the commercial banks, borrowing by the better-off developing countries played a large part in 'recycling' these funds and ensuring that they were turned into export orders for northern manufacturers. Without this, the recession of that period would have been much worse; the effect has been estimated in one study to have been comparable in magnitude to a significant reflation of the West German economy.

There is also much anxiety about the availability of raw materials, preferably cheap, from underdeveloped countries. The increases in the price of oil caused a furore, though they have certainly also been made responsible for crises which have more to do with the weaknesses of the capitalist system in general. But other commodities are also important to the West. The ILO (International Labour Organisation) reports that in

1970 the western industrialised countries obtained from underdeveloped countries 85 per cent of their bauxite, 100 per cent of their chrome, 17 per cent of their copper, 30 per cent of their iron, 95 per cent of their tin, and so on, in addition of course to nearly all of their supplies of tropical crops such as tea, coffee and bananas; it estimates most of these percentages will increase substantially by 1985. As the Brandt Report points out, the industrialised countries now produce about two and a half times as much minerals per head, including fuels, as 'developing' countries, but they consume sixteen times as much, which is why about seventy per cent of the world's imports of fuel and non-fuel minerals come from 'developing' countries; and the proportions are increasing. Not only is this dependency great, but it appears that there is insufficient new investment in raw materials extraction. This is partly because the prices paid are low and too unstable for investment to be attractive. It is also because the old arrangement, under which underdeveloped countries signed away the right to exploit their natural resources to multinational companies for the indefinite future, has broken down; the governments of underdeveloped countries are now less willing to do this and they are also attempting to nationalise existing concessions or renegotiate existing agreements, with the result that multinationals are no longer willing to take the risk of making investments and then being denied their super-profits. Which does not mean to say that these mining companies deserve any sympathy: Allende made the point to the United Nations in 1972 that Anaconda, Kennecott and the other companies exploiting Chilean copper had made more than $4,000 millions in profits over the previous forty-two years alone on an initial investment of less than $30 million. But it does provide more reasons for the financial authorities of the West to seek a recognition of the 'mutuality of interests' between North and South and a regulation of international financial transfers so that the necessary arrangements for securing supplies of raw materials can be made.

The particular problem of oil supplies has further ramifications. The West has somehow to ensure that the OPEC countries continue to produce and export quantities of oil which produce revenues beyond these countries' current financial needs, rather than preserving their reserves to ensure a steady income from oil in the future. Not even the most blatant levels of luxury consumption by the Arab elite can absorb their current oil revenues, and some of them are unwilling to undermine their position by too much redistribution of wealth internally. Therefore attractive forms of investment must be found for them abroad. Much of the oil money (so-called petrodollars) has so far been put in North American international banks and these banks, unable to lend their funds on a sufficient scale in developed countries because of the recession, have found willing borrowers in developing countries. But this, again, has created its own problems: most of the borrowers are already heavily indebted; Brazil and Mexico, for example, have debts of about $50 billion each, and an annual debt service of $6 to $10 billion; and other countries, such as South Korea, Turkey and Peru, are in the $10 billion debt category. The danger of default by the governments of underdeveloped countries looms over the international financial system, threatening to bring it down like a pack of cards. The 'recycling' of petrodollars therefore has to be organised so that it is safe as well as profitable, and this is what many of the proposals of the Brandt Report are designed to achieve.

An examination of the Brandt Report would in fact show that these latter problems are those to which it devotes the most space, and for the resolution of which it has the most detailed and concrete proposals. Thus its proposals for reform are designed first and most crucially to ensure that the existing world economic system functions smoothly. Second, if possible, the reforms are to be designed in such a way that they achieve some alleviation of extreme poverty in underdeveloped countries. But the Report, like most of the orthodox literature on development, notably omits to explain why the poverty exists in the first place. If it attempted such an explanation, it might come to the embarrassing conclusion that the poverty is caused precisely by the economic system which its proposals are supposed to protect.

Extremes of Poverty and Wealth

There is no lack of information on the extreme forms of deprivation which the majority of people in this world now suffer. Most but not all of these people live in Asia, Africa and Latin America. There are, in addition, glaring inequalities in wealth between different parts of the world and also within individual countries. The 'widening gap' between 'developed' and 'developing' countries has become a cliché. There are also a good many indications, less well documented perhaps, that the situation of the very poor, especially in rural areas in underdeveloped countries, is becoming worse in absolute as well as in relative terms, mainly because distribution within countries is becoming more unequal.

The United Nations, its agencies, and the World Bank and the International Monetary Fund compile statistics on such matters. These are full of qualifications and probable inaccuracies, but even so give some indication of the scale of the problem. According to the World Bank's 1980 *World Development Report*, the average annual income per head of 18 industrialised countries in 1950 was $3,841; that of the 38 countries with lowest incomes was $164, or about one twenty-third. In 1980 the estimated average income of the former was $9,684; the income per head of the latter was $245, or barely one fortieth. The 18 industrialised countries include the United States, Canada, Australia, New Zealand and Japan as well as Western Europe. From statistics elsewhere in the World Bank's *Report*, it is possible to calculate that in 1979 these countries, with about 16 per cent of the population of the world, received about 63 per cent of its income. The others, which include the 'low income' countries and also some 'middle income' countries, the oil exporting countries, and what the World Bank calls the 'centrally planned economies', thus have 84 per cent of the population and only 37 per cent of the income. The Brandt Commission Report puts it another way:

> The North including Eastern Europe has a quarter of the world's population and four fifths of its income; the South including China has four billion people — three quarters of the world's population but living on one fifth

of the world's income.

Figures of income per head are obviously difficult to estimate and cannot be taken as exact measurements. But they do indicate the massive differences in living standards that exist in different parts of the world; and they do not exaggerate them. The figures cannot be assumed to be wrong merely because it appears impossible that people could feed themselves on £100 a year and less. The simple fact is that most people in underdeveloped countries do not have enough to eat. People in the so-called developed countries commonly eat too much; and some live in extreme luxury. The figures moreover conceal differences within countries. The yachts and palaces are not confined to the inhabitants of the First World. Some people in underdeveloped countries are extremely rich; ex-president Somoza of Nicaragua was one of the richest men in the world. Others are correspondingly poorer; the distribution of income in underdeveloped countries is probably on the whole more unequal than that in the industrialised countries, in which considerable deprivation nevertheless exists, in spite of their overall wealth. The 1980 *World Development Report* gives some tentative figures on income distribution within countries. In Brazil the poorest fifth of the population apparently get 2 per cent of the income, and the richest fifth get 67 per cent; for Malaysia the corresponding figures were 3 per cent and 57 per cent; for India 7 per cent and 49 per cent; and for Britain 6 per cent and 39 per cent.

There are other measurements of differences between countries. The figures are, again not totally accurate, but they give some indication of the realities. According to the estimates in the *World Development Report*, the average adult literacy rate in 1975 in the 18 most industrialised countries was 99 per cent; in the 38 'low income' countries it was estimated to be 38 per cent. Average life expectancy in 1978 was 74 years in the former group and 50 years in the latter. The proportion of children of school age in secondary schools in 1977 was, respectively, 87 per cent and 24 per cent. The average daily calorie supply per head in 1977 was, respectively, 3,377 (or 131 per cent of requirements) and 2,052 (or 91 per cent of requirements). The population per doctor in 1977 was 630 in the former group and 9,900 in the latter. Again it should be noted that all these figures are national averages; doctors and food are congregated in cities. Energy consumption per head in the former group in 1978 was 7,060 (kilograms of coal equivalent); in the latter it was 161. The value of manufacturing output per head in 1976 was $3,126 in the United States, $1,640 in Britain, $293 in Chile, $63 in India and $11 in the Central Africa Republic. Wage rates in underdeveloped countries are often one twentieth to one thirtieth of those in the richer countries, for the same type of work.

The authorities of the international system also publish estimates of the total number of 'destitute' people. The estimates vary. In the early 1970s the ILO said that there were 700 million of these destitute people. Today the World Bank says that, 'excluding the centrally planned economies', there are about 800 million people, or almost 40 per cent of the population of the so-called developing countries, who live in 'absolute poverty': 'a condition of life so characterised by malnutrition, illiteracy and disease as to be beneath any reasonable definition of human decency'. In some countries one child in four dies before the age of five. Millions of people live in houses or huts made of corrugated iron, cardboard boxes and other 'impermanent' materials. They have no running water and no toilets. Electricity is a luxury. Health services are rarely within walking distance, and have to be paid for. Primary education may be available and free but often children are needed for work. There is generally no social security or unemployment pay, and many people, some 300 million according to the ILO, are without any kind of employment. Trade union rights and organisation are often minimal or non-existent and severe repression by government authorities is the rule rather than the exception.

Conventional Explanations for Poverty

Elaboration of these facts can be found in most textbooks on underdevelopment. But they usually remain unexplained; or the explanations, if given at all, are inadequate. For a start, the question addressed is not usually the question of why the international distribution of income is so unequal. Explanations are attempted to show why the peoples of underdeveloped countries are 'poor', but the existence of their poverty is not related to the wealth accumulated elsewhere. Moreover, the picture given is usually a static one, as if it is some kind of unchanging fact of nature that Indian children have stomachs bloated by malnutrition. Attempts to provide historical explanations are dismissed as irrelevant: 'focussing on questions of historical guilt will not provide answers to the crucial problem of self-responsibility', says the Brandt Report.

The explanations, such as they are, tend to be based on what might tactfully be called a Eurocentric view of the world, which is itself a product of historical circumstances, and of colonial mythology in particular. Europeans, who began by being impressed and indeed overawed by what they found in civilisations sometimes more sophisticated than their own, gradually built up theories of racial superiority. Especially from the nineteenth century onwards, they felt the need to justify to themselves their domination of the colonial peoples, and in particular the institution of slavery. The 'natives', they maintained, were lazy, stupid, barely human. An Englishman in 1820 found the cause of Indian poverty 'in a natural debility of mind, and in an entire aversion to labour'. By the nineteenth century, says V. G. Kiernan in *The Lords of Human Kind*, 'the white man had worked himself into a high state of self conceit'. White men were willing to justify everything to themselves in the cause of bringing 'civilisation' to the natives. 'An opium smuggler', says Kiernan, 'who could not help feeling shocked when he saw the "shrivelled and shrunken carcasses" produced by the drug, landed on one occasion on Formosa with his men, had a fight, burned a village, plundered a junk, and removed its ammunition because "there was no knowing how much they might yet require, before the natives were brought into submission to our superior civilisation".' The British Opium War to force the Chinese authorities to allow the importation of opium was justified by John Quincy Adams, in a public lecture in 1842, in the following terms:

> The moral obligation of commercial intercourse between nations is founded entirely, exclusively, upon the Christian

precept to love your neighbour as yourself …But China, not being a Christian nation … admits no obligation to hold commercial intercourse with others … It is time that this enormous outrage upon the rights of human nature [i.e. China's refusal to buy opium] … should cease.

Africans were thought to have a 'worse than Asiatic idleness' (though one adminstrator, quoted by Kiernan, says: 'the natives think we are lazy dogs, but very clever at making the black man do our work'). Europeans thought that it must be a blessing for African slaves to be provided with masters and regular work and consoled themselves with the idea that 'Negroes have far duller nerves and are less susceptible to pain than Europeans.'

Europeans convinced themselves that they were the bearers of order, civilisation and Christian principles to the benighted natives. 'In carrying out this work of civilisation,' said Joseph Chamberlain in 1897,

we are fulfilling what I believe to be our national mission, and we are finding scope for the exercise of those faculties and qualities which have made of us a great governing race … No doubt, in the first instance, when these conquests have been made, there has been loss of life among the native populations, loss of *still more precious* lives among those who have been sent out to bring these countries into some kind of disciplined order, but it must be remembered that this is the condition of the mission we have to fulfill. [emphasis added].

'I contend,' said Cecil Rhodes, one of the biggest empire-builders,

that we are the first race in the world, and that the more of the world we inhabit the better it is for the human race … If there be a God, I think what he would like me to do is to paint as much of the map of Africa British red as possible.

Such ideas survive and permeate our consciousness today. Hugh Trevor-Roper, Regius Professor of History at Oxford University, has maintained that 'the history of the world, for the last five centuries, insofar as it has significance, has been

European history.' Europeans are still, of course, convinced that they know best. 'Aid' agencies are eager, if not arrogant, with their advice to poor countries on how to 'catch up' and how to overcome 'backwardness', and the development expert business has developed into a massive gravy train for the experts. Multinational companies sell themselves as the purveyors of technology and efficiency; 'even if local governments were strong and assistance to them plentiful,' says Herbert C. Cornuelle in the 1968 Annual Report of the United Fruit Company, 'the fact is that the enormous complexities of the development process require abilities and attributes which are as natural to the multinational corporation as they are unnatural to government.' And the President of General Foods (GFC) boasts:

> What is it that GFC can contribute to a foreign subsidiary? Well, first we have more than 10 per cent of all the food researchers in private industry in this country, and therefore we have a capability in food technology to contribute. Our Dream Whip and Gainsburger dog food products, for example, were technical achievements.

Failure to develop is put down to 'lack of entrepreneurs'. Thus Professor Yale Brozen holds that 'efficient technological advance ... requires a supply of innovating entrepreneurs checked or goaded by a free market.' Walter Elkan, whose Penguin book *Introduction to Development Economics* is in all libraries and is widely available, writes that 'development depends on having people who are enterprising', although elsewhere in the book he recognises that much of the supposed reluctance of peasants to innovate is based on rational economic decisions. Writers on the economics of underdeveloped, or 'backward', countries still argue seriously that people in these countries are poor because they live in hot climates and imply that this makes them lazy and, therefore, lacking in enterprise.

The reality is much more complex. It has been argued that in 'the original affluent society' people did not suffer want or hunger and that they did work less. But whatever may have been the diversity of cultural patterns in the past, it is clear that today many people in underdeveloped countries work far longer hours in far worse conditions than people in the West. In Hong Kong, for example, many thousands of people work over 100 hours a week and many thousands of children also work. Peasants, who form the great majority of the population of underdeveloped countries, are in the fields from dawn until dusk; they work 12- to 15-hour days, seven days a week. Borlaug, a pioneer of the Rockefeller-promoted 'Green Revolution' (see p. 58 below) says: 'I have a lot of respect for the small farmer ... Almost invariably when you look at what he's doing with his land, you find he's producing the maximum under the situation he has to work with. The thing is he usually doesn't have much to work with.' As for the supposed lack of entrepreneurs, it is the case that hard-headed, coldly calculating, ruthlessly profit-maximising people are to be found in all parts of the world. The materials with which they work, and the social and economic framework in which they operate, differ.

Another 'explanation' for the extreme poverty of under-developed countries is 'lack of capital'. This, like the 'low level equilibrium trap' of neo-classical economics jargon, amounts to saying that they are poor because they are poor. An Oxford don, wishing to be helpful, said to the Indian post-graduate student sitting next to him: 'We have the capital and you have the men', and suggested that the two should be brought together. With rather more subtlety, the Brandt Report says: 'fundamental structural changes must be made in the markets in which developing countries are suppliers — of commodities, of manufactures, of labour — and in which they are customers — for capital and technology.' But this begs the question of what constitutes capital. It also fails to answer the question why developed countries have the 'capital' or indeed whether, in any but the narrow sense of having access to it and control over it, they have it at all. The Brandt Report is clear that 'a foreign company need not always bring capital with it, for it can borrow in local markets'. This is a mild statement of a situation in which, according to some estimates, foreign businesses commonly raise around 80 per cent of their capital in underdeveloped countries while at the same time remitting their profits abroad. In addition, because the distribution of income in underdeveloped countries is so unequal, much of the capital which could otherwise be available for investment is squandered in extravagant living, property speculation and Swiss bank accounts. Baran, who in *The Political Economy of Growth* elaborated on these phenomena, adds that 'where the situation is nothing short of outrageous ... is in the British colonial empire'. The colonies were forced to accumulate, between 1945 and 1961, sterling balances of £1 billion, which constituted a direct export of capital to support the British standard of living, the value of the pound and Britain's ability to repay its war debts. This, of course, is merely one, relatively recent, example of a widespread phenomenon which should at least cast doubt on the 'capital shortage' theory as an adequate explanation for underdevelopment.

Then there is the population theory. People in under-developed countries are said to be poor because their populations have been increasing too fast. This, in turn, is said to be the result of superior medical techniques introduced by Europeans. These have, of course, produced undeniable benefits. They have been relatively recent. The first irruption of Europeans, particularly into North and South America, decimated many local populations, partly through exhaustion in mines and plantations, partly by introducing the Europeans' diseases, and partly by outright massacre. As late as the nineteenth century, the British exterminated the population of Tasmania. And during the period of the European slave trade the population of Africa declined substantially, so much so that some writers ascribe the relative lack of development in Africa during this period to the decline of its population and the shortage, in particular, of able-bodied men and women. Since then, the population of the world has been increasing dramatically. It is now about 4.3 billion; over the next two decades it is likely to increase by nearly two billion, which is more than the total population at the beginning of the twentieth century.

The current alarms about populations are filled with Malthusian over-tones. It is too easy to ascribe poverty to natural, unchangeable causes and then to say that nothing can be done about it. Malthus himself provided comfort to British industrialists paying starvation wages at the beginning of the nineteenth century by telling them that population was bound to increase at a geometric rate, whereas production could, by the nature of things, increase only at an arithmetic rate; and so, if the workers starved, it was their own fault for breeding too fast and they must practise abstinence. Malthus was proved wrong in Britain. But, as far as the underdeveloped countries are concerned, the latter-day Malthusians are at it again.

Highly popular writers like W. Vogt, in his *Road to Survival*, can say that, unless the 'untrammelled copulation' of 'spawning millions' is brought to an end, 'we might as well give up the struggle' and, incidentally, we must get rid of the 'sort of thinking ... that leads to the writing and acceptance of documents like the Communist Manifesto ... It tricks man into seeking political and/or economic solutions', whereas our environment is 'as *completely* subjected to physical laws as is a ball we let drop from our hands.' [emphasis added] 'Also', said Vogt in 1948,

> there is little hope that the world will escape the horrors of extensive famines in China within the next few years. But from the world point of view, these may be not only desirable but indispensable. A Chinese population that continues to increase at a geometric rate could only be a global calamity.

Another writer, R.C. Cook, in *Human Fertility: the Modern Dilemma*, foresees that, in addition to the other problems of growing population, there will be 'a steady decrease of the percentage of the earth's population which subscribes to the ideas and culture patterns evolved in the Western world since 1600' and 'badly distributed fertility will result in ... speeding the erosion of our biological and cultural heritage'. Baran, from whom these quotations are taken, insists in his book *The Political Economy of Growth* that they are not the product of a lunatic fringe. It is partly because birth control programmes are associated with such views that many people in underdeveloped countries are rightly suspicious of them.

There is another rather sinister twist to the question. This is that birth control methods which are widely accepted to be unsafe in developed countries are nevertheless foisted on the peoples of underdeveloped countries. There is good evidence to show that the United States AID (Agency for International Development) and US drug companies maintain a systematic and deliberate double standard for the sale of contraceptives. Unsafe IUDs, high-estrogen birth control pills and, recently, Depo-Provera, which has been pronounced unfit for use in the United States, have been bought up cheap by the USAID from the drug companies, which cannot dispose of them in the United States, and widely distributed in underdeveloped countries. An official of an AID-funded birth control programme, sensitive to charges of racism, proposed that Depo-Provera might be approved for use in the United States:

> I'd like to suggest that [in the United States] you can find sub-groups of people who have the same problems as people in the Third World. They may not be so large, but you know you have several million immigrants from Mexico, who bring with them the same health problems, the same cultural assumptions, the same need for fertility regulation as they had in Mexico. I think that if the FDA were to turn its attention to the needs of some of the sub-groups in the United States, we would not be faced with the situation in which we can be accused of having a dual standard of medical practise and drug regulation around the world.

In Britain, too, Depo-Provera has been used on women in low income groups in Glasgow and on women from ethnic minorities. A medical textbook published in London says that: 'for the average individual in a Western country, depot progestagen preparations have a limited use (because of the medical risks associated with it)'; but for 'various psychiatric patients', 'drug addicts', and 'the underdeveloped world', the method would be 'suitable'.

It is not clear how much rapid increases in population do, in fact, add to the difficulties in providing reasonable standards of living. In the early stages of the industrial revolution in Europe, population was increasing quite rapidly. Some highly industrialised countries have population densities much greater than those in most countries where there are extremes of poverty. Many calculations show that food supplies in the world as a whole are more than adequate, actually and potentially, to feed a population much larger than the existing population, although, as Susan George in her book *How the Other Half Dies* puts it, it would obviously 'not be ecologically desirable to decimate the last natural forest in order to provide arable land and food for tens of billions of people'. Rapid population increases cause particular problems at particular times, but it is the case that in many countries with the greatest problems of malnutrition *overall* food supplies have been increasing faster than the increase in population. This is so for nearly all countries in South and East Asia, including India; moreover, as a study by Keith Griffin and Ajit Kumar Ghose argues, the faster population increased, the faster agricultural production increased. They suggest that the most likely explanation for probably increasing impoverishment in rural areas is not to be found in population increases, but rather in an increasingly unequal distribution of income.

Many governments have decided that they should make attempts to limit population increases. These attempts have possibly been most systematic and successful in China, where the predicted famines have in any case not occurred. Without mentioning that the state government has for many years been controlled by communist parties, the Brandt Report gives the example of the successes in the Indian state of Kerala. It ascribes these successes to the fact that people have been 'involved in the workings of government', that health and education programmes have been widely spread, and that adequate food supplies have been assured for the poor. Other underdeveloped countries, Sri Lanka for example, have effective programmes of birth control.

Historically, birth rates have tended to decline with improvements in living standards, as they have in Europe and North America. This is not to say that population increases cause no problems or that they can necessarily be left to take care of themselves. It is simply to point out to the apologists of the existing world order that 'untrammelled copulation' is not the problem.

It is tempting to add that, if population is to be considered the problem, then it is perhaps the populations of the developed countries that might need controlling since, according to some estimates, they and their animals consume over half of the available world supply of food grains. Feeding grain to animals is a wasteful way of producing proteins for humans to eat. A quotation from Rene Dumont is one possible epitaph on the population argument:

> The rich white man, with his overconsumption of meat and his lack of generosity for poor people, behaves like a veritable cannibal — an indirect cannibal. By consuming meat, which wastes the grain that could have saved them, last year we ate the children of the Sahel, Ethiopia and Bangladesh. And we continue to eat them this year with undiminished appetite.

But this is part of a wider argument, which has to do with the question whether, rather than saying that the poor should be blamed for their poverty, it might not be truer to say that the problems lie with the rich, those who expropriate the fruits of the labour of the poor.

> Once upon a time there was a little chimney sweep, and his name was Tom ... He lived in a great town in the North Country, where there were plenty of chimneys to sweep, and plenty of money for Tom to earn and his master to spend. (Charles Kingsley, *The Water Babies)*.

The Past is Not Irrelevant

It is very hard to understand the present situation of underdeveloped countries without some reference to their past. The accumulation of wealth in Europe and North America, and their industrial and technological advance, are relatively recent phenomena. It was in the nineteenth century, with the Industrial Revolution, that the huge advances in first British and then other European, North American and later Japanese wealth and productive capacity took place. Even so, during most of the nineteenth century the situation of working people in Europe was in its own way as bad as anything anywhere. Children were removed from the cities to the mills at the age of seven or eight; they worked in factories for up to 12 or 15 hours, standing throughout. 'They always strapped us if we fell asleep,' testified an eleven-year-old boy, who is quoted in Leo Huberman's book, *Man's Worldly Goods*.

That standards of living for working people in Europe

were precarious at the beginning of the twentieth century is brilliantly shown in Robert Tressell's novel, *The Ragged Trousered Philanthropist*. Even today there are places within industrialised countries where poverty is severe, including the United States where the principles of free enterprise are most resolutely upheld; in 1972 the US Bureau of Census stated that 'at least 10 to 12 million Americans are starving or sick because they have too little to eat.' But throughout the last two centuries there have been slow gains in the strength and organisation of the European and North American working class, against the vigorous resistance of the state and employers, and it cannot be denied that their situation now is incomparably better than it was in the nineteenth century, and than it still is for workers and peasants elsewhere.

The change in the relative position of Europe can be said to have begun about five centuries ago when European traders and adventurers began their expansion overseas. Empires and civilisations have risen and declined and the European empire, though long-lasting, was only the latest of many. In fact the growth of what some might call civilisation came rather late in northwest Europe and later still in what is now the United States. Before then, the major centres of power, wealth, the development of luxurious living, cities, monuments, a division of labour, science and technology, and whatever else may be the attributes of 'civilisation', were to be found elsewhere. This does not mean that there was some kind of Golden Age before the Europeans made their impact. Earlier empires were oppressive and of course hierarchical and much of what they did was no doubt as brutal as what their peoples subsequently suffered under the Europeans. Slavery was practised on a large scale by the Arabs. The Aztecs practised human sacrifice. The Europeans burned witches. It is obviously very difficult to compare the degree of oppression and deprivation suffered then and now. But what is clear is that the Europeans did not, at that time, possess anything that might be termed superior civilisation, or even superior techniques, on a world scale. The latter developed later, in ways that have to be explained.

The earliest empires were in China, India, what are now North Africa and the Middle East, later in Greece and Rome. Northern Europe began to emerge from its backwardness in the

Middle Ages. Its contact with the more advanced civilisations of the East was at first through the merchant cities of Italy, which traded through the intermediary of Islamic merchants. In the thirteenth century Marco Polo went to China and was staggered by the richness of the civilisation he found there; he brought back glowing accounts which inspired later expeditions in search of the wealth of the East. In the eleventh and twelfth centuries the Crusaders, supposedly motivated by the desire to restore the Holy Land to Christendom, had already whetted the appetite of Europeans for the luxuries of the East. But Europeans, at that time, had little to offer in return, except silver, which was scarce.

Woytinsky and Woytinsky, in their book *World Commerce and Governments*, say that at the beginning of the period of European expansion,

> Europe lagged behind Asia in industrial skill. In exchange for silk, cotton, sugar and spices, Europe could export only small arms, which were hardly any better than those made in the East ... The superiority of commerce, handicraft and administration in China in comparison with Italian cities was the theme of the fascinating story Marco Polo told ... His story relates to the end of the thirteenth century, but there is no indication that Europe was catching up with China in the following century and a half.

As late as 1793 the Emperor of China wrote to King George III, as follows:

> As your Ambassador can see for himself, we possess all things. I set no value on objects strange or ingenious, and have no use for your country's manufactures.

A similar situation existed in India. The Woytinskys write:

> After having landed in 1498 at Calicut, on the Malibar coast of India, Vasco da Gama returned with a friendly letter from the Raja of Malabar to the King of Portugal. 'In my kingdom there is abundance ... What I seek from thy country is gold, silver, coral and scarlet.'

Throughout the world there were civilisations whose level

of organisation and degree of wealth was highly advanced: in Egypt, Persia, Benin, the Maghreb, Ethiopia, Java, Angkor. In Peru and Mexico there were vast ceremonial stone buildings, some of which survive; the Inca civilisation in Peru had forms of social security which somewhat resembled a modern welfare state. In Africa there were comparable developments; Walter Rodney, a Guyanese historian who was recently murdered for his political activities in Guyana, gives many examples in his book, *How Europe Underdeveloped Africa*; thus, he quotes from Dutch visitors to the city of Benin in the fifteenth century:

> The town seems to be very great. When you enter into it, you go into a great broad street, not paved, which seems to be seven or eight times broader than the Warmoes Street in Amsterdam ... The king's palace is a collection of buildings which occupy as much space as the town of Harlem ... There are numerous apartments for the prince's ministers and fine galleries, most of which are as big as those on the exchange at Amsterdam ... These people are in no way inferior to the Dutch as regards cleanliness; they wash and scrub their houses so well that they are polished and shining like a looking glass.

Elsewhere there were other, less developed forms of state organisation. But the existence of more or less complex forms of the state in many parts of the world before the period of European expansion means that there were also, of necessity, a division of labour, specialisation in the production of certain goods, and a development of new techniques of production. In India, the skill which was most clearly more developed than in Europe was the manufacture of textiles whose quality was much superior to that produced elsewhere. Indians had also advanced in other fields, for example in the iron and steel industry. In Africa there were highly developed techniques of working in bronze, including the much admired Ife and Benin bronzes of the fourteenth and fifteenth centuries; there were sophisticated forms of exchange based on gold mined in Africa; and there were well developed trade networks, for example across the Sahara between North and West Africa. A superior brand of red leather, which became known to Europeans as 'Moroccan leather', was tanned and dyed by Hausa and Mandinga specialists in what are now northern Nigeria and Mali. There were fine local cloths made of bark and palm fibre, which had a finish like velvet; and cotton cloth was also widely manufactured, specialisation taking place in the various stages of its production. North Africa was on the whole more highly developed than the rest of Africa; in particular, it was responsible for some of the scientific discoveries on which later European progress was based. There was trade between the Incas and the Aztecs before the arrival of the Spaniards, mainly in metals and luxury goods.

It is difficult to determine whether the capacity of people to feed themselves was greater before the period of European expansion than it is now. It seems that, in the earliest societies of hunters and gatherers, and slash and burn agriculture, there was little hunger. But famines existed before the advent of the Europeans, and famines have been made, by hoarding and greed, from the earliest times. The Romans used North Africa as a granary for their population. But the organisation of dominated areas into producers for the requirements of others has taken place, as will be seen, on a much larger and more systematic scale over the last four centuries. What is clearly the case is that, in a number of areas, self-sufficiency in food and also the fertility of the soil have been destroyed; and people have become dependent, to a degree that did not exist before, on buying food which often they cannot afford.

It may thus be the case that the widespread and chronic malnutrition of the type that exists today in many parts of the world is a relatively new phenomenon. Josue de Castro, in *The Geography of Hunger*, gives numerous examples to indicate that nutritional levels have deteriorated in many areas. Walter Rodney argues that:

> Colonialism created conditions which led not just to periodic famine, but to chronic undernourishment, malnutrition and deterioration in the physique of the African people. If such a statement sounds wildly extravagant, it is only because bourgeois propaganda has conditioned even Africans to believe that malnutrition and

starvation were the *natural* lot of Africans from time im-
memorial. A black child with a transparent rib-case, huge
head, bloated stomach, protruding eyes, and twigs as arms
and legs was the favourite poster of the large charitable
operation known as *Oxfam* ... *Oxfam* never bothered
[the] consciences [of the people of Europe] by telling them
that capitalism and colonialism created the starvation, suffering and misery of the child in the first place.

That Oxfam has changed its policy since Rodney wrote his
book does not, of course, alter his case.

What also probably needs saying, because of the widely
held assumptions that Europeans have been helping the peoples
of underdeveloped countries to escape from their backwardness, is that agriculture in many parts of the world was quite
highly developed before the period of European expansion, in
some areas more so than it is now. In Asia the state authorities
in India, China, Sri Lanka, Kampuchea and other places had
built elaborate irrigation systems and hydraulic works, many
of which have subsequently fallen into disuse. A.J. Voelker, a
British agricultural scientist assigned to India during the 1890s,
wrote:

Nowhere would one find better instances of keeping land
scrupulously clean from weeds, of ingenuity in device of
water-raising appliances, of knowledge of soils and their
capabilities, as well as of the exact time to sow and reap, as
one would find in Indian agriculture. It is wonderful, too,
how much is known of rotation, the system of 'mixed
crops' and of fallowing ... I, at least, have never seen a
more perfect picture of cultivation.

In Africa, agriculture was not as advanced as it was in
Asia and Europe, partly because of the mainly communal
organisation of land tenure which assured everybody of sufficient land and partly because of the overall abundance of land.
Even so, advanced methods were well known and used, for
example, terracing, crop rotation, green manuring, mixed
farming and regulated swamp farming. It was only when the
colonialists intervened that the agricultural devastation, so
familiar today, began.

The Europeans Get Ahead

The questions that need to be answered, then, are why, from about 1500 onwards, prodigious advances began to take place in Europe, and why the situation elsewhere deteriorated. The first thing to be said is that the two phenomena are obviously related; how much so, is a matter of controversy. Second, enough may by now have been said to make it fairly obvious that there is no justification for racist explanations of the causes of European domination. Otherwise why did civilisations develop elsewhere earlier than they did in Europe?

What is distinctive about the European advance is not just that from the end of the fifteenth century onwards they began to expand overseas and eventually to dominate large areas of the world, but that they also were the first to develop the form of production known as capitalism. Capitalism reached its fully fledged form in Britain in the nineteenth century, but the first moves towards a factory system in Britain are to be found earlier; Jack of Newbery set up a factory early in the sixteenth century. And in the seventeenth and eighteenth centuries, agriculture in Britain became increasingly capitalist, in the sense that the land was concentrated into relatively large farms on which people worked for wages. The main distinguishing feature of capitalism is that it is a form of production in which the tools, materials and the land necessary for producing goods are no longer owned by the people who do the work, but by capitalists who employ labourers for a wage. In the earliest forms of social organisation, each family or group provided for its own needs. Specialisation and a division of labour grew up later, at first in the form of individuals working in their own houses to produce particular goods, then, as in the guild system in mediaeval Europe, in small workshops in which craftsmen worked with their own tools and usually sold directly to the public. The organisation of wage labourers into factories and mills made possible much greater efficiency in production, partly because mechanisation could be introduced on a much larger scale and also because jobs could be broken down into simple, repetitive components and performed much more rapidly by a relatively unskilled workforce. Eventually in nineteenth century Britain, goods, notably textiles, could be produced on a mass scale much more cheaply than they could be by skilled artisans working in small workshops, many of which were put out of business. This, of course, is a process which continues today, even within the industrialised countries.

It is easier to understand why capitalism, once it had developed, became such a productive and dominant system, than it is to explain why it first developed in Britain. All kinds of different explanations are given, most of them rather partial and unsatisfactory, some of them so specific that it's difficult to see them as other than chance factors rather than part of any coherent theory. But some indications of where explanations may lie can perhaps be given, and may, by implication, help to explain why such developments did not take place elsewhere. It is fairly generally agreed that, for capitalist forms of production to develop, two main conditions are necessary: a 'free' labour force and the accumulation of money capital in the hands of potential investors. In Britain such a labour force became available, from the fifteenth century up to the nineteenth century, mainly as a result of 'enclosures' and evictions of small peasants in order to increase the size of holdings. Small farmers and tenants were deprived of their means of subsistence when landlords found that it was profitable to enclose what had previously been common land and to take over small farms, often in order to use the land for grazing sheep and producing wool. Thus were created large numbers of people who had 'nothing to sell but their labour-power'. The history of enclosures was punctuated with peasant revolts. In the words of one rebellious jingle of the time:

> The law locks up the man or woman
> Who steals a goose from off the common;
> But leaves the greater villain loose
> Who steals the common from the goose.

Eventually many of those made landless found jobs in the new industries of the industrial revolution. At first the numbers of landless labourers thus created were, from the fifteenth century onwards, greater than the numbers of jobs created in new industries. Draconian laws were therefore introduced against vagabondage and the state at first had little difficulty in helping employers to keep down the level of wages. In fact employers were sometimes supplied with what amounted to forced labour in the form of vagabonds who could escape execution if somebody was willing to put them to work as virtual slaves. Elizabeth I decreed in 1572:

> Unlicensed beggars above 14 years of age are to be severely flogged and branded on the left ear unless someone will take them into service for two years; in case of a repetition of the offence, if they are over 18 years of age, they are to be executed, unless someone will take them into service for two years; but for the third offence they are to be executed without mercy as felons.

Laws against vagabondage and loitering, designed to keep the unemployed off the streets, persisted into the nineteenth century and included the 'sus' laws — revived in the 1970s and widely used against young blacks.

So much for the 'rosy dawn of capitalism'. But what about the money for the capitalists to invest? Their apologists claim that they were virtuous, frugal people who saved out of their hard work in order to invest for greater returns in the future. One of the things the Protestant Reformation did in Britain was to reverse the previous moral imperatives; usury was no longer sin but virtue. Thus the Puritan, Baxter, asserted:

> If God show you a way in which you may lawfully get more than in another way (without wrong to your soul or to any other), if you refuse this, and choose the less gainful way, you cross one of the ends of your calling, and you refuse to be God's steward, and to accept his gifts and use them for him when he requireth it; you may labour to be rich for God, though not for the flesh and sin.

And Calvin wrote: 'What reason is there why the income from business should not be larger than that from landowning? Whence do the merchant's profits come, except from his own diligence and industry?' In fact, they come from the labour of his workers. And before the workers could be put to work, some initial capital, or wealth, was required.

Much of this initial wealth came, not from the frugality of individuals, but from the new gains to be made in overseas trade — a term which included conquest, piracy, and plunder. As Marx summarised the process in the first volume of *Capital*:

> The discovery of gold and silver in America, the extirpation, enslavement, and entombment in mines of the aboriginal population, the beginning of the conquest and looting of the East Indies, the turning of Africa into a warren for the hunting of black skins, signalised the rosy dawn of the era of capitalist production. These idyllic proceedings are the chief momenta of primitive accumulation.

One reason the Europeans went trading and plundering overseas may have been precisely their own relative lack of wealth and the greater desirability of the products available overseas, especially in the East. But in the process, and especially after their search for another route to the East led them to the discovery of gold and silver in America, they themselves began to accumulate considerable wealth.

The question of course remains why this wealth, in Northern Europe and especially in Britain, was invested in industry, whereas elsewhere it was not, or not to the same extent. Spain and Portugal did not use the massive riches they obtained in America to invest in industry. And arguably there was more wealth available in India and China than there was in Europe throughout this period. One explanation is that the social order in Northern Europe was relatively weak and unstable. In Britain the serfs had obtained their freedom from many of their obligations to landlords after the Black Death. Wars between nation states in Europe were endemic and their monarchies needed money to wage them. They came increasingly to rely on borrowing from the new merchant and banking classes. In return they were willing to support them in their overseas ventures and eager to participate in their profits. They also supported them in undermining the entrenched rights of landlords and the restrictive monopolies of the city guilds, thus giving them the freedom they needed to embark on new forms of production. This freedom was not available to other merchants elsewhere who were repeatedly crushed by powerful absolutist states, such as the Islamic, Chinese and Indian, who taxed and confiscated their fortunes. Their rulers were determined to ensure that no rival source of power arose; hence the Chinese prohibition of the Indian Ocean trade. The power of these states, in turn, was based on a prosperous agriculture whose advanced forms of irrigation needed and supported a considerable labour force. They were relatively self-sufficient and therefore there was less inducement for them to trade or to support the activities of traders.

The explanations put forward for the early development of capitalism in Britain need not imply that capitalism could not have developed elsewhere as a result of internal changes in existing societies; they merely suggest why it might first have developed where it did. There are examples of incipient forms of capitalist production to be found in many parts of the world before capitalism developed in Europe: textile factories in Byzantium, mines in Moslem Spain, mining and metal-working factories in China. Mao Tse-Tung, for instance, argued that: 'China would have (therefore) even without the impact of foreign capitalism gradually developed into a capitalist country.'

Whatever the historical peculiarities of industrial development in Britain, the crucial question is what effect this had on development elsewhere. The conventional wisdom is, as has been said, that the British and other colonial powers have helped the rest of the world to escape from the backwardness in which they found them, or to which they were doomed by the failings of their societies, if not by the inherent weaknesses of their peoples. A variant of this view is held by some marxists, who would denounce any imputations of 'inherent weaknesses', but who would nevertheless say, following Marx, that the metropolitan powers, by introducing capitalist forms of production into backward and feudal areas, in fact played a progressive role. Thus many marxists have expected societies elsewhere to go through the same sort of processes, warts and all, that have been experienced in the industrial development of Britain and other countries.

Some, on the other hand, have argued that the effect of European expansion into other parts of the world has been to thwart and stunt the development that would otherwise have taken place. They have argued that foreign intervention, far from helping countries to develop, has *produced* under-development. Most countries in the world have long since been incorporated into the capitalist world market, but this has not led them to develop fully either capitalist relations of production or, in general, their productive capacity, especially in industry. On the contrary, it has destroyed existing forms of industrial activity and introduced hunger where it did not exist before. André Gunder Frank, possibly the most famous proponent of the thesis of the 'development of underdevelopment', argues that:

> Contemporary underdevelopment is in large part the historical product of past and continuing economic and other relations between the satellite underdeveloped and the now developed metropolitan countries.

Many other writers have taken up these ideas. Walter Rodney, for example, says:

> The developed and underdeveloped parts of the present capitalist section of the world have been in continuous contact for four and a half centuries. The contention here is that over that period Africa helped to develop Western Europe in the same proportion as Western Europe helped to underdevelop Africa.

It is sometimes argued that the effect of external forces on the impoverishment of the underdeveloped countries has been exaggerated, and that the local ruling classes should be blamed instead. The answer is obviously that underdevelopment is a product of a combination of external and internal forces. The question of relative degrees of responsibility is difficult to determine. But it is also the case that the nature of the local ruling classes has itself been influenced by external domination. The colonial powers and their successors have commonly allied themselves with the most reactionary forces within under-developed countries and have helped to crush resistance to them, in the past and also today. For example, when the Western powers invaded China in 1856-60, they did so not only to impose a new trade treaty; General Gordon's mercenaries also helped the Chinese ruling class to suppress the Taiping Rebellion, on the grounds that a Taiping victory would have resulted in a reformed and centralised China which would have been better able to resist European penetration. In Africa and Asia the Europeans ruled through making use of and reinforcing pre-existing power structures, removing recalcitrant kings and emirs, transforming local rulers into 'Native Princes', and 'Native Authorities', or simply 'chiefs', who were subordinate to and dependent on their colonial overlords but whose powers over their own subjects were often reinforced and extended by the colonial authorities. The latter extended their power and defended it by a conscious policy of divide and rule, to weaken resistance and the development of nationalist movements. Sometimes they imposed reactionary social structures where they did not exist before. The Spaniards introduced various semi-feudal forms of land ownership into Latin America which still act as powerful barriers to progress today. In Latin America and in other colonised areas, the colonial and post-colonial powers sometimes deliberately maintained or actually reinforced pre-capitalist forms of production in order to avoid the necessity of paying full subsistence wages to workers in plantations and mines. In India the East India Company transformed the *zamindaris* or tax-farmers of the Mogul Empire into land-owners and handed over whole provinces to them. The process continues today, with many 'pro-Western' governments being dependent for their survival on outside support. They and their foreign backers have combined to produce a world order which clearly is disastrous for the great majority of the peoples of the underdeveloped countries.

Proponents of the 'development of underdevelopment' thesis usually go on to argue that the nature of the underdeveloped countries' relations with developed countries is such that it is no longer possible for development to take place in the former under capitalism, and that the only means of escape from underdevelopment is socialism. Even if the full development of capitalism is eventually possible for most if not all countries in the Third World, it could also be argued that, especially in the Third World, the costs of such development in human hardship are unacceptably high and that it may be possible for such countries to attempt immediately to build more just and humane forms of society.

But whatever the conclusions to be derived from these ideas, it is clear that the world economic system, over the past four hundred years, has become increasingly integrated and that international economic relationships have had a powerful effect on what can and cannot be achieved within particular societies. The argument here is that, although external domination has not necessarily prevented the development of capitalism in the Third World in the past and may not do so now, it has hindered and distorted such development and increased its costs, and still does so today. The fact that capitalism was established first in Northern Europe gave Europe decisive advantages in its dealings with other countries. If there had been no foreign domination of the countries that are now underdeveloped, they might well have developed faster and with less hardship for their peoples.

Plunder and Loot

Adam Smith, the classic proponent of the arguments for free trade and an authority resorted to by many latter-day apologists for Empire, wrote in *The Wealth of Nations* of the early days of European expansion:

> A new set of exchanges, therefore, began to take place which had never been thought of before, and which should naturally have proved as advantageous to the new, as it certainly did to the old continent. The savage injustice of the Europeans rendered an event, which ought to have been beneficial to all, ruinous and destructive to several of those unfortunate countries ... To the natives both of the East and West Indies, all the commercial benefits which can have resulted from these events have been sunk and lost in the dreadful misfortunes which they have occasioned.

Much of what goes under the heading of 'trade', especially in the early days of European expansion, amounted to little more than plunder. Europeans coveted the wealth of the East. They obtained the means to pay for it — at first gold and silver and later, more indirectly, slaves — largely by <u>force.</u> The Spanish and Portuguese found gold in South America; the British, who had failed to find any gold in North America, got it from the Spaniards, at first by piracy on the high seas and later by selling them slaves. Slaves were obtained partly by armed raids or exchanged for rum and guns. The first trading posts in Asia and elsewhere were often established by force. When the British East India Company had defeated the Muslim rulers of Bengal in 1757, it obtained the local cloth, in the words of an English merchant, 'by every conceivable form of roguery ... fines, imprisonments, floggings, forcing bonds from them, etc.'.

The expeditions in which Europeans 'discovered' America, beginning with Columbus's expedition in 1492, had as their purpose to reach the fabled riches of the East by a Westerly route, thus by-passing Arab intermediaries and avoiding the long trade-routes across Asia. Columbus and his successors were certainly brave and intrepid explorers, and they went with all kinds of blessings from monarchy and Church. But what they were after was money. Adam Smith says:

> The pious purpose of converting [the inhabitants] to Christianity sanctified the injustice of the project. But the hope of finding treasures of gold there was the sole motive which prompted them to undertake it ... The first English settlers in North America ... offered a fifth of all the gold and silver which should be found there to the king, as a motive for granting them their patents.

When Cortes advanced towards Mexico, Montezuma sent envoys to him with gifts of golden collars. According to a Mexican text preserved in the Florentine Codex, the Spaniards were in 'seventh heaven':

> They lifted up the gold as if they were monkeys, with expressions of joy, as if it put new life into them and lit up their hearts. As if it were certainly something for which they yearn with a great thirst. Their bodies fatten on it and they hunger violently for it. They crave gold like hungry swine.

Later when they reached Tenochtitlan, the splendid capital with 300,000 inhabitants, the Spaniards entered the treasure house,

> and then they made a great ball of the gold and set a fire, putting to the flames all that remained no matter how valuable, so that everything burned. As for the gold, the Spaniards reduced it and made bars.

So the first purveyors of European 'civilisation' were philistines, as well as 'hungry swine' and 'monkeys'. They were also violent and treacherous. In Peru, Pizarro extracted a ransom of a roomful of gold and two of silver from the Inca Atahualpa; and then he strangled him. The European thirst for gold and silver culminated triumphantly in the discovery of Potosi, the 'mountain that gushed silver'. They put the natives, those that were left after the ravages of conquest, to work extracting it, and most of them died.

Europeans had set out to obtain, as well as gold, the pepper, ginger, cloves, nutmeg and cinnamon, silk and other textiles from Asia. Though America turned out not to be India, its discovery had the incidental advantage of providing them with the means to trade in Asia. They used the gold and silver which they plundered in America to buy what they could not plunder in Asia. The Europeans had little of their own to offer the industrially more advanced and self-sufficient Chinese and Indians, who clearly were military powers to be reckoned with. Thus, at first, Europe's trade with the East was relatively peaceful. It was carried on at the expense of the ravages and wholesale murder they were committing in America.

Plantations, Workers and Slaves

These ravages were further extended with the introduction into that continent of sugar, cotton and tobacco plantations. The Europeans eventually introduced the plantation system into nearly all the areas they dominated to grow the products they wanted. But it was first introduced in America. The first chapter of Eduardo Galeano's book *The Open Veins of Latin America* is entitled 'Lust for Gold, Lust for Silver'. The second is dedicated to 'King Sugar and Other Agricultural Monarchs'. Sugar was then scarce and highly prized in Europe. On his second voyage to America, Columbus planted sugarcane roots in the Dominican Republic. The plantation system spread throughout the Caribbean and, notably, to the Brazilian northeast. Land was granted by the monarchs to individual conquerors and soldiers and the present-day latifundio system evolved from these original grants of land. Galeano says:

> The land was devastated by this selfish plant which invaded the New World, felling forests, squandering fertility, and destroying accumulated soil humus. The long sugar cycle generated a prosperity as mortal as the prosperity generated by the silver and gold of Potosi.

The absorption of land by plantations and latifundios progressed fast and the local people were left with less and less land to provide for their own needs. Of the Brazilian northeast, now notorious as a vast area of semi-starvation, Galeano says:

> The humid coastal fringe, well watered by rains, had a soil of great fertility, rich in humus and mineral salts and covered by forests from Bahia to Ceara ... Where everything had bloomed exhuberantly, [European colonisation] left sterile rock, washed-out soil, eroded lands.

With their grants of land, the conquerors received the Indians who lived on the land: Cortes, for example, received 23,000 vassals. But their numbers were soon decimated by hard work, European diseases, and outright massacre. Estimates of the numbers killed by the Spaniards in the Americas range from 12 million to 15 million; densely populated regions like Haiti, Cuba, Nicaragua and the coast of Venezuela were completely depopulated. The Portuguese in India behaved in similar fashion; prisoners were slaughtered and their hands, noses and ears sent in mockery to the 'barbarian' kings. The availability of labour was a problem for colonialists everywhere, and they resorted to the use of slaves.

The Dutch in the East Indies, for example, had man-stealers specially trained to obtain slaves from the Celebes for use in their plantations in Java. But the shortage of labour was most severe in the Americas and new supplies were sought in Africa. Thus began the biggest of all the slave trades, and the one in which the British were the major operators. Estimates of the number of African slaves who reached America alive range from 10 million to over 100 million. To this figure must be added the 15 to 20 per cent killed on the journey, the many more killed while resisting capture and the many killed in the wars waged between Africans to obtain captives for sale to Europeans. The ones chosen were of course the young and the able-bodied, and the places from which the slaves mainly came (the Congo, Eastern Nigeria and Dahomey) were among the most highly developed. Africa was transformed into a hunting ground for slaves; few parts of Africa, even those remote from the West coast, escaped the influence of this savage form of 'trade'. Slaves were sometimes sold and re-sold as they travelled from the interior to the coast, and the African economies were disrupted by war. Walter Rodney says that, although slaves were undoubtedly purchased, 'on the whole, the process by which captives were obtained on African soil was not trade at all. It was through warfare, trickery, banditry and kidnapping.' Local rulers and elites were transformed into accomplices of the 'trade'; and in return for slaves, the products that were offered were rum, guns and textiles.

The institution of slavery continued in the Americas up to the nineteenth century, in particular because of the need of British industry for cotton grown in North American plantations. In 1828 the following advertisement appeared in the *Charleston Courier*: 'as valuable a family ... as ever was offered for sale, consisting of a cook about 35 years of age, and her daughter about 14 years and son about 8 years. The whole will be sold together or a part of them, as may suit a purchaser.' As Marx commented, the institution of free wage-labour in Europe was built upon the pedestal of slavery in the Americas.

Profits

These various forms of activity, loosely defined as trade, were highly profitable. The British started off their accumulation with piracy but the biggest profits were to be made in the slave trade. As Professor H. Merivale put it in a lecture at Oxford University in 1840:

> What raised Liverpool and Manchester from provincial towns to gigantic cities? ... Their present opulence is as really owing to the toil and suffering of the Negro as if his hands had excavated their docks and fabricated their steam engines.

And Walter Rodney says:

> The actual dimensions are not easy to fix, but the profits were fabulous. John Hawkins made three trips to West Africa in the 1560s, and stole Africans whom he sold to the Spanish in America. On returning to England after the first trip, his profit was so handsome that Queen Elizabeth I became interested in directly participating in his next venture; and she provided for that purpose a ship named the *Jesus*. Hawkins left with the *Jesus* to steal some more Africans, and he returned to England with such dividends that Queen Elizabeth made him a knight. Hawkins chose as his coat of arms the representation of an African in chains.

After the British won the Battle of Plassey in India in 1757, their attention shifted to a great extent from the West Indies to India. The famous Bengal Plunder began to arrive in London soon after, and its arrival coincided with what is generally considered to be the beginning of the industrial revolution in Britain. It has been estimated that the total British plunder of India between 1757 and 1815 amounted to £1,000 million; the national income of Britain in 1770 was about £125 million. Direct tribute payments alone through the East India Company approximated £1 million in some years. Ernest Mandel, in his book *Marxist Economic Theory*, adds up the value of the gold and silver taken from Latin America up to 1660, the booty extracted from Indonesia by the Dutch East India Company from 1650 to 1780, the harvest reaped by French capital in the eighteenth-century slave trade, and the profits from slave labour in the British Antilles and from a half-century of British looting in India. These, Mandel says, are only the most substantial amounts for which figures, of a sort, are available. But they add up to over a billion pounds sterling, or 'more than the capital of all the industrial enterprises operating by steam which existed in Europe around 1800'. For Britain alone, the profits from operations in the West Indies and India between 1760 and 1780 was probably more than double the amount of money available to invest in the new industries of the industrial revolution.

The money thus extracted by trade and plunder in the countries that are now underdeveloped may not have been directly invested in industry, and may, as some have argued, have been used mainly for luxury consumption, land purchase and the further expansion of trade. But some of it certainly found its way into industry through the banking system if not directly. It thus provided part of the money needed to get the process going.

Markets and the Destruction of Industries

But this was, of course, not all. The overseas activities of the British obtained for them the raw materials, in particular cotton, that were essential for the expansion of industry. It also provided markets. Once the British had built their industries, they found that they needed outlets for them beyond the restricted markets that were available domestically. British industry grew rapidly at the end of the eighteenth century. It could not have done so if it had not been able to export. At the end of the seventeenth century British exports were about five per cent of the value of national income; a century later they were about 15 per cent; and by the end of the nineteenth century they had reached a peak of over a third of national income. At the beginning of the industrial revolution, about 70 per cent of British exports went to the territories that the British dominated. As Eric Hobsbawm puts it: 'the cotton industry was thus launched, like a glider, by the pull of the colonial trade to which it was attached.'

The search for new markets continued to motivate expansion through the nineteenth century and still does so today.

Here is a nineteenth-century view of the matter, put forward by Henry Morton Stanley on his return from meeting Livingstone in the middle of Africa. In a speech to British industrialists he said:

> There are forty millions of people beyond the gateway of the Congo, and the cotton-spinners of Manchester are waiting to clothe them. Birmingham foundries are glowing with the red metal that will presently be made into iron-work for them and the trinkets that shall adorn those dusky bosoms, and the ministers of Christ are zealous to bring them, the poor benighted heathen, into the Christian fold.

Stanley's 'trinkets' have their modern equivalents. These days, a large proportion of the production of many of the biggest and best-known companies is for export, and more than a third of the exports of industrialised countries go to what are now the underdeveloped countries. Many of these exports are of course useful. But some of the products currently pressed upon the peoples of underdeveloped countries involve the creation of artificial 'needs' through advertising, and some are, as the forcing of opium into China was, downright harmful; for example, scented soap powder may replace the more effective local scrubbing soap; white bread and other refined food, which dangerously reduce the fibre intake in people's diets, may replace traditional types of food; babies die because their mothers are convinced by advertising that Western powdered milk must be 'better'; cigarettes with a high tar content and drugs that are banned in developed countries are dumped in underdeveloped countries.

The new interest of the British in markets for the products of their industry had other consequences for the rest of the world. It meant the more-or-less deliberate destruction of their industries. As early as the seventeenth century, when the British began enacting the protective Navigation Acts, colonies were prohibited by law from turning to any industry which might compete with the industry of the mother country. For example the North American colonists were forbidden to manufacture caps, hats, woollen or iron goods. They were expected to send the raw materials for these products to England to be manufactured and then to buy them back from England. The same rules applied to other British colonies. When the Irish attempted to make their wool into cloth, their cloth industry was prohibited by British laws; moreover, their wool could only be exported to England, at prices dictated by the English, who then re-exported what they didn't want themselves.

In Africa, Europeans had already undermined much of the local textile industry by bringing in textiles from India, thus adding to the destruction of African commerce, mining and industry already wrought by the slave wars. These Indian textiles, in Africa and also in America, then began to be replaced by textiles from Britain.

One of the more notorious facts of British colonial history is that the British subsequently proceeded to destroy the industrial economy of India itself. Between 1815 and 1832 the value of Indian cotton goods exported fell from £1.3 million to below £100,000. Not only that, but the value of English cotton goods imported into India rose from £156,000 in 1794 to £400,000 in 1832. By the middle of the nineteenth century India was importing a quarter of all British cotton exports. The British eliminated competition from Indian textiles through an elaborate network of restrictions and prohibitive duties. Even within India, taxes effectively discriminated against local cloth. The resulting hardship was great for the Indian weavers; and it was also eloquently protested against by the East India Company, whose trading profits were suffering. Sir Charles Trevelyan declared to a parliamentary enquiry in 1840:

> The population of Dacca has fallen from 150,000 to 30,000 or 40,000 and the jungle and malaria are fast encroaching upon the town ... Dacca, which used to be the Manchester of India, has fallen off from a flourishing town to a very poor and small one.

'The bones of the weavers,' wrote a Governor-General of the East India Company in 1835, 'are bleaching the plains of India.' Not only the textile industry but the iron and steel industry was destroyed as well. The duties imposed on Indian exports into Britain were, in spite of the 'free trade' doctrines being promoted at the time, five to twenty times higher than the duties that were allowed on British imports into India. And the destruction was completed by physical means where necessary.

In Egypt, the British followed a similar policy. As Lord Cromer, who governed Egypt from 1883 to 1907, put it:

> The policy of the government may be summed up thus: (1) export of cotton to Europe ... ; (2) imports of textile products manufactured abroad ... : nothing else enters into the government's intentions, nor will it protect the Egyptian cotton industry, because of the dangers and evils that arise from such measures ... Since Egypt is by her nature an agricultural country, it follows logically that industrial training could lead only to neglect of agriculture while diverting the Egyptians from the land.

Twenty-five years later, Cromer looked back on the results of his policy:

> The difference is apparent to any man whose recollections go back some ten or fifteen years. Some quarters [of Cairo] that formerly used to be veritable centres of varied industries — spinning, weaving, ribbonmaking, dyeing, tentmaking, embroidery, shoemaking, jewellery making, spice grinding, copper work, the manufacture of bottles out of animal skins, saddlery, sieve making, locksmithing in wood and metal, etc. — have shrunk considerably or vanished. Now there are coffee houses and European novelty shops where once there were prosperous workshops.

Free Trade and Comparative Advantage

There thus began the gradual process of the conversion of the dominated territories into markets for the products of European industry and suppliers of raw materials and primary commodities. This is made to appear to be their natural destiny, an idea Marx poured scorn on in his *Discourse on Free Trade* written in 1848:

> We are told, for example, that free trade will give rise to

an international division of labour that will assign each country a production that is in harmony with its natural advantages. You may think, Gentlemen, that the production of coffee and sugar is the natural destiny of the West Indies. Two centuries earlier, nature, which is unaware of commerce, had not placed either coffee trees or sugar cane there ... If the free traders cannot understand how one country can enrich itself at the expense of another, we should not be surprised, since these same gentlemen do not want to understand either that within a country one class can enrich itself at the expense of another.

The theories of free trade and comparative advantage have held powerful sway in the West. They are propounded as a scientific explanation of reality but they are, in fact, ideological tools.

Adam Smith, Ricardo and their 'neo-classical' successors produced their theories on free trade only after the British had established their industrial preeminence. In the early days of British industrialisation, industrialists sought and obtained protection for their 'infant' industries against competition from abroad. Here is a plea from an early British manufacturer:

I have now, I think, shewn, Sir, that the linen manufacture ... is but in its infancy in Britain and Ireland, that therefore it is impossible for our people to sell so cheap ... as those who have had this manufacture long established among them, and that for this reason, we cannot propose to make any great or quick progress in this manufacture, without some public encouragement.

For a considerable period the British, by means which were sometimes far from 'natural', not only destroyed the long-established industries of others, but protected their own from competition. Friedrich List, who argued in the 1840s for the protection of nascent German industry against competition from the by then established British industries, wrote, after reviewing the benefits derived by Britain from the protection of the Navigation Acts:

England therefore *prohibited* the articles competing with those of her *own factories*, the silk and cotton goods of the

East. This prohibition was absolute and under severe penalties, she would not consume a thread from India ... Their policy has been attended by the most splendid success ... What would have been her condition, had she purchased for these last hundred years the cheap goods of India?

As the economic historian Carlo Cipolla notes:

It is fortunate for England that no Indian Ricardo arose to convince the English people that, according to the law of comparative costs, it would be advantageous for them to turn into shepherds and to import from India all the textiles that were needed.

Once British industry was established, it was safe to argue the virtues of Free Trade. Similarly, these days, the United States government and the International Monetary Fund argue that it must be beneficial for all countries to open their doors to imports; but there are signs that, with United States fears for their industrial competitiveness, a change of theory among the (North American) gurus of neo-classical economics is on the cards; and in Britain it is again becoming almost respectable to argue openly for import controls, as the Cambridge Economic Group does, to protect declining British industries.

It would be wrong to suggest that Adam Smith, much of whose work is brilliant and perceptive, crudely or dishonestly set out to serve the interests of British industrialists. Nevertheless his theories did accord with what British capitalists needed in 1776, when his famous book, *The Wealth of Nations*, was published. His support for the idea of free trade was based on the argument that specialisation and a division of labour brought about great increases in productivity, that a wide market was necessary to make a division of labour possible, and that the market should therefore be broadened by free trade. He argued against all preferences or restraints for particular forms of economic activity, and for 'the obvious and simple system of natural liberty' as the method of increasing the real wealth and greatness of society.

David Ricardo extended the argument on free trade:

Under a system of perfectly free commerce, each country

naturally devotes its capital and labour to such employments as are most beneficial to each. This pursuit of individual advantage is admirably connected with the universal good of the whole. By stimulating industry, by rewarding ingenuity, and by using most efficaciously the peculiar powers bestowed by nature, it distributes labour most effectively and most economically: while, by increasing the general mass of productions, it diffuses general benefit and binds together, by one common tie of interest and intercourse, the universal society of nations throughout the civilised world. It is this principle which determines that wine shall be made in France and Portugal, that corn shall be grown in America and Poland, and that hardware shall be manufactured in England.

Such ideas had, and still have, a phenomenal amount of influence on people's thinking. And yet they were quite clearly incorrect, even at the time. The fact that Portugal concentrated on wine was not at all the result of the natural workings of the market. It was imposed by the British government, in particular in the Methuen Treaty of 1703 whose provisions were specifically aimed to increase British textile exports to Portugal and Portuguese wine exports to Britain. This treaty, which more or less finalised Portuguese economic dependence on Britain, was preceded by a number of other commercial treaties in which Portugal ceded economic advantages to Britain in return, principally, for military protection against Spain.

A particularly blatant example of the use of force to impose 'free trade' was the Opium Wars against China. The Chinese government had attempted to ban the importation of opium and also imposed duties on imports of manufactured goods. In 1840 the British fleet attacked China and the result was a series of treaties granting foreigners special privileges in so-called Treaty Ports, the cession of Hong Kong, the lowering of duties, and eventually the legalisation of the opium trade.

The use of force to open up new markets was common practise. The international division of labour that resulted in Britain becoming, for much of the nineteenth century, the dominant industrial power was clearly not simply the result of 'natural' economic forces, but was imposed by the substantial exercise of political and economic force at times by the state. Where trade on 'normal' commercial terms was not possible, colonisation and direct rule were resorted to. And when, towards the end of the nineteenth century, Britain's industrial preeminence was threatened by other European powers, they and Britain again embarked on another process of colonisation, this time mainly in Africa, in order to obtain for themselves protected markets abroad. This struggle for markets led the Europeans to fight among themselves, and culminated in the first world war of 1914-1918. Thus it came about that G.K. Chesterton could boast:

> The earth is a place on which England is found
> And you find it however you twirl the globe round;
> For the spots are all red and the rest is all grey,
> And that is the meaning of Empire Day.

Or, as Hilaire Belloc put it,

> Whatever happens, we have got,
> The Maxim gun, and they have not.

Hunger

The inexorable conversion of the dominated areas into markets for European manufactured goods and suppliers of primary commodities and raw materials for European consumption undermined not only their previous self-sufficiency in manufactures, but also, increasingly, their ability to feed themselves. As Baran comments, the problem is not a division of labour as such, but 'an intra-national and international specialization that is so organised that one participant of the team specializes in starvation while the other assumes the white man's burden of collecting the profits.' Colonies were converted into virtual plantations (or mines) producing one or two crops (or mineral products) for export to Europe.

In the process, Europeans took much of the best land. This happened on a massive scale, especially in America and Africa. Lord Delamere got 100,000 acres of the best land in Kenya at a penny per acre. The amount of land available for subsistence, in other words for the production of food for local consumption, was drastically reduced and is still decreasing in many parts of the world. The local people were forced into native reserves (as in some parts of Africa) or onto difficult and mountainous terrain (as is the case all over the Caribbean and Latin America and also in India, especially in the South). The land left for subsistence was too intensely cultivated and began to be exhausted and eroded, and the plantations themselves often had a devastating effect on the natural fertility of the land.

Josue de Castro says, in *The Geography of Hunger*:

In Africa it is not only because it cuts down local production of foodstuffs that the regime of production is ruinous to the natives, but also because it exhausts the soil by intensifying the factors of erosion. This has happened ... with monkey-nut growing in Senegal.

The 1951 Report of the Kandyan Peasantry Commission in Ceylon, says Ernest Mandel in *Marxist Economic Theory*:

explains how the monoculture of coffee and tea, and the uncontrolled deforestation, brought about ecological damage which was the fundamental cause of the serious floods experienced in 1957.

And: 'In Egypt the extension of cotton-growing and the practise of permanent instead of periodical irrigation caused a rapid exhaustion of the soil.' It also apparently caused a rapid increase of diseases in the Nile Valley. And: 'In the period between 1934-35 and 1939-40, the area of India's soil under food crops declined by 1.5 million acres, while during the same period the area under export crops increased in the same proportion.'

More examples are to be found from other sources. In Gambia, rice farming was widespread before the colonial era, but so much of the best land was given over to groundnuts that rice had to be imported on a large scale to try to avoid famine. In India, the South was turned into a plantation economy not dissimilar to the Latin American ones. According to Palme Dutt, the exports of raw cotton rose from 9 million lbs in 1813 to 32 million lbs in 1833, 88 million lbs in 1844 and then to 963 million lbs in 1914. Exports of tea and of food grains, mainly rice and wheat, rose from £858,000 in 1849 to £19,300,000 in 1914. India thus became a major exporter of wheat to Europe. As Sir George Watt wrote in 1908, 'the better classes of the community were exporting the surplus stocks that formerly were stored against times of scarcity and famine.'

In Latin America the spread of the plantations began producing hunger at an earlier time. Sugar was succeeded by other crops, in particular rubber, but the sugar plantation remains the archetype. Galeano describes the Cuban experience:

In the years following British occupation ... the sugarmills absorbed everything, men and land. To the mills went shipyard and foundry workers and the countless small artisans who had contributed decisively to the development of industry. Small peasants growing tobacco ... or fruit ... ,victims now of the canefields' brutally destructive advance, also turned to sugar production. Extensive plantation relentlessly reduced the soil's fertility; sugar towers multiplied in the Cuban countryside and each one needed more and more land ... Dried meat, a Cuban export a few years earlier, was by 1792 arriving in large quantities from abroad and was an import from then on. The shipyard and foundry languished, tobacco production plummeted; the slaves put in a workday of up to 20 hours. On smoking lands the 'sugarocrasy' consolidated its power ... Early chroniclers told of travelling across all of Cuba in the shade of giant palms and through leafy forests abounding in mahogany, cedar and ebony. Cuba's precious woods may still be admired in ... Madrid, but in Cuba the sugarcane invasion sent the best virgin forests up in smoke. In the same years it was destroying its own timberlands, Cuba became the chief purchaser of United States timber. The extensive plunder-culture of sugarcane meant not only the death of the forest but also, in the long run, the death of the island's famous fertility. With forests surrendered to the flames, erosion soon did its work on the defenseless soil and thousands of streams dried up.

This process is continuing in many parts of the world. The desert in West Africa is spreading. With the growth of refrigeration the number of food crops that can be exported for luxury consumption in the developed countries has increased. In Upper Volta peasants have organised themselves into unions to demand the right to grow food crops for themselves rather than vegetables for export to France. Ernest Feder, in his book with the self-explanatory title *Strawberry Imperialism*, gives a detailed account of the process in Mexico. Under the heading 'ASEAN is becoming a vegetable plot and fishpond for the developed world', Ho Kwon Ping in the *Far Eastern Economic Review* describes how the commercial production of pineapples, bananas and other tropical fruits for export has displaced local farmers, giving employment for some of the new landless at $1 or $2 a day and in grim conditions, and how Thai exports of seafood have doubled over recent years, while production has remained stable, so that local consumption of fish had declined. Africa is currently a net *exporter* of barley, beans, peanuts, fresh vegetables and cattle; in Mali peanut exports to France increased notably during the years of drought. Mexico supplies the United States with over half of its supply of several winter vegetables, and half of Central America's agricultural land produces food for exports.

Obviously the production of food and other commodities for Europeans did not always result in a drastic reduction of subsistence areas. In some parts of the world there was abundant land so that agricultural production for export could take place without reducing the amount of food available locally; and food shortages in Africa, in particular, are quite recent. But there are enough examples of the opposite to make it a significant factor in the patterns of hunger that exist today. Particularly in recent years, many countries, some of them the same ones that are exporting massively to Europe, North America and Japan, have become heavily dependent on imports of food for barest survival. For example, according to the World Bank's *World Development Report*, in the late 1970s food constituted 40 per cent of the imports of Sri Lanka, 19 per cent of Mali's, 30 per cent of Senegal's, 23 per cent of Egypt's, 17 per cent of Malaya's, 13 per cent of Mexico's; a good deal more than most of them spent on oil. Not only countries, but also individuals living in rural areas as well as in towns, have become precariously dependent on *buying* food and are deprived of the basic security of being able to produce for themselves. As a Nigerian farmer said at the time of the 1974 famine: 'in the Great Famine of 1914 we had money but no food; now we have food but no money.'

Although famines are not only a modern phenomenon, there are some indications that they have increased in intensity and depth. In India there appears to have been a drastic increase in deaths from famine from 1800 onwards, with at least 16 million people dying of hunger in the nineteenth century, nearly all of them in the last quarter of the century. The deaths resulting from the Great Bengal Famine of 1943, according to A.K. Sen, amounted to as many as three million. Sen says that there was no significant decline in the amount of food available in that year compared to previous years in which there were no famines; the problem was that people in rural areas in Bengal did not have the money to buy it. The food went to Calcutta, and also out of Bengal: it went in fact where the money was. There are stories of destitute people, who had trekked into Calcutta in search of food, dying in front of full shop windows. Sen gives some similar evidence to show that the famines in Ethiopia in 1973 and 1974, which were responsible for the deaths of between 50,000 and 200,000 people, were not the result of overall food shortages in Ethiopia as a whole, but of a terrible decline in the purchasing power of people in the areas affected by the famines.

In general it is clear that a very important factor contributing to hunger is the unequal distribution of food and the money to buy it. As has been said earlier, this inequality is increasing. The colonial powers have tended to reinforce the power of landlords or, as in the cases of Latin America and Africa, to create new landlords. In India peasants have become deeply indebted to money-lenders and traders who are able to force them to sell their crops cheaply in order to obtain further credit. Such traders hoard food and sell it in times of scarcity at prices that peasants cannot afford. Although overall food production may be potentially adequate for everybody in countries such as India, the food is disproportionately available to the rich, especially in towns or in prosperous areas. There is much evidence that this increasing inequality means not only that the rich are getting richer, but also that the poor are getting poorer and therefore more malnourished.

In the last twenty years or so, there has been what is called in the West a 'Green Revolution', which has been promoted as a solution to the problems of underdeveloped countries. It has consisted mainly in the development of new high-yielding varieties of seeds. What the Green Revolution does not do is solve the problems of distribution. There have certainly been considerable increases in overall food production in a number of underdeveloped countries, especially in Asia. But the increases have not been distributed to those who need them and malnutrition persists. An ILO study shows that in the seven largest South Asian countries the rural poor are worse off than they were 10 or 20 years before; it notes that, ironically, 'the increase in poverty has been associated not with a fall but with a rise in cereal production per head, the main component of the diet of the poor.'

The Green Revolution was born in Mexico in the 1940s in the context of the need to get more food to the cities. As Moore Lappe and Collins explain:

> All effort went to the development of a capital-intensive technology applicable only to the relatively best-endowed areas or those that could be created by massive irrigation projects. The focus was on how to make seeds, not people, more productive. True rural development based on making each rural family productive and better-off would have meant that the rural majority itself would have eaten much of any increment in food production. This increment was exactly what the ascendant urban interests counted on taking *out* of the countryside.

This pattern has persisted. The Green Revolution, as it is practised by the agencies of the West and the governments they support, has been described as a policy of 'backing the best'. The inputs — of fertiliser, pesticides, irrigation, machinery and good land required to make the miracle seeds produce their miracle yields — are beyond the reach of most small farmers, who have little or no access to credit; and the whole thing bypasses the landless. In fact there is plenty of evidence that the numbers of landless are increasing as a result of the greater profitability of agriculture: land-owners mechanise production and evict their tenants; farms in the Punjab, according to a World Bank study, grew by 240 per cent in three years in the 1960s. The new demand for fertilisers, pesticides and machinery, which has been created by the adoption of Green Revolution seeds, has also resulted in bigger markets for the major agribusiness firms which have become increasingly important in the multinationals' league. This factor no doubt also partly explains the eagerness with which the techniques of the Green Revolution are promulgated in official circles.

Workers and Wages

The problem of finding workers for the mines and plantations was a continuous one. Professor Merivale, in lectures delivered around 1840, relates how a certain Mr Peel took out to Australia with him:

> three hundred individuals of the labouring classes; but they were all fascinated by the prospect of obtaining land ... and in a short while he was left without a servant to make his bed, or to fetch him water from the river.

'Shed a tear for Mr Peel,' Huberman comments, 'who had to make his own bed simply because he did not realise that as long as workers have access to their own means of production — in this case, the land — they will not work for someone else.'

Where the Europeans did not themselves take over the ownership of the land they needed to persuade local people to produce for the market, rather than for their own consumption. There were some cases, for example in what is now Ghana, in which local farmers quite eagerly grew cash crops in order to obtain access to imports. Often, however, the 'natives' were not eager either to produce export crops or to work on the estates of Europeans. In some places, in particular in the Caribbean and in South America, they were simply not available in sufficient numbers, and African slaves were imported. Even after slavery was abolished in the nineteenth century these continued to provide a more or less captive labour force. An eyewitness wrote from the Brazilian northeast:

The human cattle market was open as long as there was hunger, and there was no lack of buyers. Rare was the steamer in which large numbers of Ceara people were not shipped out.

Elsewhere the problem was more complicated. In Africa itself there are examples of Africans being forced to work for Europeans, or to grow cash crops, by gun and whip. The best known of these examples were in Tanganyika under German rule, in Portuguese colonies right up to the period of the liberation struggle, and in French Equatorial Africa and the French Sudan in the 1930s. The use of more-or-less open forms of forced labour was widespread; the British made use of the practise up to the second world war.

But possibly the most usual way of getting Africans and others to produce cash crops was to exact tribute or taxes; these had to be paid either in the cash crop desired or in money which could only be obtained by selling crops or by working for Europeans for a wage. This meant of course that the time and land that could be devoted to producing food was reduced and that subsistence farming was deprived of many able-bodied men and women. Migration became a massive phenomenon in Africa in particular. According to one official account, the *Keiskammahock Rural Survey*, concerning the Ciskei region of South Africa:

The people of this district are ... seen to be dependent upon the earnings of emigrants for their very existence, and it is poverty which forces them out to work. But this very exodus is itself a potent cause of the perpetuation of the poverty at home, for the absence of so many in the prime of life inhibits economic progress and certainly accounts in no small measure for the low agricultural productivity of the district. In many cases land is not ploughed for the simple reason that there is no one to do the ploughing.

The inducement to work in European mines or farms was also sometimes reinforced by deliberate attempts to depress living standards in subsistence areas. A contemporary example of a business reaction to a problem of excessive prosperity among potential workers is to be found in the *Seventh Annual Report of the Chamber of Mines of Rhodesia*, whose president observed in 1902:

> With this cheap form of [family] labour at his command, coupled with the fact that, provided he lives on Native Reserves, he has no rent to pay, and that his taxation is reduced to a minimum, the native is enabled year after year to produce a large amount of grain, which is in due course purchased from him by the trader, and eventually at an enhanced price by the mine owner, and in fact he continues year after year to become more affluent, less inclined to do any work himself, and to enter most successfully into competition with the white man in that most important of articles, namely, grain. I would suggest that a remedy can be found in two ways, namely, by taxation and the adoption of a co-operative system of farming by the mine owner.

It has also been argued, by Jack Woddis in *Africa, the Roots of Revolt*, that Europeans took land, which they did not cultivate, for two purposes: to make sure that Africans could not compete with Europeans, and also so to impoverish them that they were forced to go to work for Europeans. That this also had its problems for the Europeans is shown by this quotation from Lord Lugard, Governor-General of Nigeria:

> The problem of today is to ensure that service with Europeans shall not result in the premature disintegration of native society. For the illiterate worker who has lost faith in the approval or anger of his forbears, who has renounced his tribal loyalties and his claim to a share in the family or clan land and the ready help of his fellows in time of need, has now no motive for self-control and becomes a danger to the state.

Europeans were concerned not only with obtaining raw materials and agricultural commodities, but with obtaining them at very low cost. Therefore the wages paid to workers and the prices paid to peasant producers had to be as low as possible. Slaves were of course not paid at all, although they had to be fed and sheltered, more or less. After the formal abolition of slavery (which was not everywhere effective), hunger drove them to work for a pittance — a situation graphically and movingly described in the novels of B. Traven.

One method of keeping down wages was to make sure that, although wages might provide for the bare subsistence of the workers themselves, the cost of providing for them in old age or sickness and of providing for the children who would supply the next generation of workers, was borne not by their employers or by the state, but by others. Lord Haley, for example, put this quite clearly in 1938:

> The reserves are used as 'shock absorbers' in the sense that they satisfy the needs of the unemployed, the sick, the old without cost to the state ... There is no other alternative except that of a permanent labour force installed in the cities around the mines and factories and completely separated from the land; but such a labour force would need higher wages, adequate housing, schools, entertainment and social security.

This system was applied widely to workers in colonial areas, especially in Latin America and Africa, and still applies to the situation of migrant workers in Southern Africa and elsewhere. It has its modern variants too, although Lord Haley's idea that a workforce cut off from the land would need social services and so on has not been too rigidly adhered to. Multinational companies, especially those currently manufacturing consumer goods in 'low wage areas' for consumption in the rich countries, pay wages that are a fraction of those paid to workers in rich countries; pick and choose among workers; use women, children and apprentices; take them at their fittest; sack them when they are worn out; and leave the euphemistically-termed 'informal section' in the slums of the cities to take care of any other needs they or their families may have. Thus they are freed of many of the charges that employers and state are expected to take on in the developed countries. There is perhaps another parallel in the so-called 'brain drain': underdeveloped countries produce and train doctors and other skilled personnel, who are then used in the developed countries without the cost of training them or of supporting them when they are not working.

The result, over the years, of the various methods of assuring the availability of cheap labour in the dominated areas has been that very large numbers of people are separated from their means of subsistence, are landless or severely impoverished, and have no alternative to seeking employment in the 'modern' sector of the economy. Massive unemployment, underemployment and migration from impoverished rural areas into cities in search of employment have become the most obvious features of current forms of underdevelopment.

Thus the use of forced labour, the more-or-less deliberate impoverishment of rural areas, the bare subsistence wages that could be paid to migrant workers because their families remained on their own small plots of land, the small and dispersed labour force, the pool of landless and unemployed people created by colonial policy — all these factors have made it possible for Europeans and now for the multinational companies of the West to pay extremely low wages in what are now the underdeveloped countries.

Attempts to organise trade unions were, and are, crushed. The colonial states, which rested on the use of superior force, remained absolutist; the same is true of many, if not most, post-colonial states. Whereas by the mid-twentieth century workers in Europe and the United States had managed to win some rights and some improvement in conditions and wages, in the colonial and semi-colonial areas conditions remained similar to those of super-exploitation which existed in the earlier stages of European industrialisation. The hours worked are very long, safety legislation is minimal, the use of child labour is increasing and, above all, wages are a fraction of the wages paid in Europe and North America and to Europeans overseas. Nigerian coalminers at Enugu in the 1930s were paid one shilling per day for working underground and 0/9d per day for jobs on the surface, which meant that European coalminers could earn in an hour nearly as much as the Enugu miners were paid for a six-day week. In Southern Rhodesia agricultural workers rarely received more than 15/- per month; and unskilled labourers in the mines of Northern Rhodesia often got as little as 7/- per month. Wage rates per day in sub-Saharan Africa reported in 1957 by the ICFTU (International Confederation of Free Trade Unions) ranged from US$0.22 (in Nyasaland) to US$0.80 (in French Somaliland and the Belgian Congo); in the

Netherlands they were US$3.50 a day, in the USA, US$10. To-day wage rates in underdeveloped countries are still commonly less than US$1 per day.

It is sometimes argued that the differences can be accounted for by differences in productivity. But the fact is that they exist even when the physical output per worker is the same as, or higher than, in similar industries in the developed countries. To the extent that there are differences in productivity, it could be argued that these are not the cause but the result of low wages: workers who are very badly paid may produce less because they eat badly, because their (badly paid) parents could not afford to send them to school, and so on. Levels of productivity depend also on levels of mechanisation and there is less incentive for employers to introduce it when wages are low. Moreover there is evidence that, even when there have been increases in productivity, wages have not increased; in fact they have remained static over long periods. The main explanation for low wages in underdeveloped countries today lies simply in the fact that there are large pools of underemployed and poverty-stricken people in rural areas and of unemployed people in towns.

Such disparities in wage levels have given rise to the idea of 'unequal exchange' as an explanation of underdevelopment. This theory has been enunciated in particular in Arghiri Emmanuel's now classic book *Unequal Exchange*, and it has been much elaborated upon, and much disputed, since the book was first published in 1969. The arguments are complicated and clearly cannot be resolved here. But the theory suggests that, since the exports of underdeveloped countries are produced at very low wages and their imports of mainly manufactured goods from Europe and North America are produced at higher wages, the exchange is an unequal one. Samir Amin, in *Accumulation on a World Scale*, has made quantitative estimates of the amounts transferred in this way. He says that: underdeveloped countries got $35,000 million for their exports in 1966; allowing for differences in productivity which were much less than differences in wage rates, they would have got an extra $22,000 million if their workers had been paid at the rates prevalent in the developed countries; and this amount is about equal to the underdeveloped countries' total investment.

The argument has been much disputed on the grounds that low wages tend to lead mainly to higher profits for capitalists, rather than to lower prices which are determined only partly, if at all, by the level of wages. For example, the world market price for rice is the same whether the rice is produced in the United States or in Burma. On the other hand consumer goods that are produced at very low wages in underdeveloped countries are usually sold cheaper than those produced in developed countries, and ordinary consumers in developed countries do benefit from these lower prices. In addition it can be argued that the low wages paid to workers in underdeveloped countries amount to a transfer of capital from underdeveloped countries to developed countries in the sense that many of the employers whose profits are thereby increased are foreigners who transfer the profits abroad.

Marxists argue that the exploitation of labour is the source of profits, or of what marxists call 'surplus value'; profits in metropolitan countries have tended to decline because of higher wages and because mechanisation has meant that wages form a lower proportion of the cost of production; this decline has been counteracted by exploiting cheap labour in underdeveloped countries. But from this it cannot be deduced that the workers of poor countries would benefit from a reduction of wages in developed countries. Emmanuel, quoting from Lenin, wrote of an 'aristocracy of labour' in developed countries; and an ecology group in France is apparently arguing for wage cuts to benefit the Third World. But as Bettelheim, one of his principle critics, says in an article in *Monthly Review*:

> When, in a capitalist country with developed productive forces, the workers do not receive higher wages, this results not in an improvement in the living conditions of workers in poor countries, but in larger profits for the capitalists of the rich ones, and so *in an acceleration of uneven development*.

In other words by making their bosses better off they would merely be helping them to strengthen their domination of the rest of the world.

Terms of Trade

Another way of looking at unequal exchange is to say that it involves the exchange of goods produced at a low level of technology with goods produced at higher levels of technology. Those in possession of higher levels of technology are likely to have an advantage and to be able to command higher prices for their products, just as skilled workers can get higher wages than unskilled workers.

The division of labour between developed and underdeveloped countries was imposed by a variety of means, as has been suggested. Once it is imposed, it is difficult to escape from it. Developed countries, or rather their business interests, are unwilling to share their technology; trade secrets are jealously guarded and technology, to the extent that it is transferred at all, is as far as possible transferred in bits or in forms which are difficult to use outside the narrow purposes for which they were designed. Markets are dominated by the big companies of the developed countries and it is difficult for newcomers to enter them. The prices charged for manufactured goods are to some extent monopoly prices, and in any case they rise steadily over time.

The governments of developed countries still exert pressures on underdeveloped countries to open their markets to the manufactured goods of developed countries, for example through the imposition of conditions on loans from the International Monetary Fund (IMF); yet they themselves put up barriers against 'cheap imports' from underdeveloped countries which might compete with their own manufacturing industries. They also impose discriminatory tariffs, quotas and freight rates to deter underdeveloped countries from processing their primary products before they export them; UNCTAD (the United Nations Conference on Trade and Development) has calculated that in 1975 the semi-processing of ten commodities could have added $27 billion to export earnings, or more than one-and-a-half times what they now earn. When Brazil in the 1960s tried to export processed coffee, the US government, acting on behalf of the instant coffee companies, threatened to cut off aid.

Representatives of the developed countries still insist that it is good for underdeveloped countries to concentrate on primary products. 'If development is to take hold,' said Kissinger in 1976 at the fourth UNCTAD in Nairobi, 'a special effort must be made to expand the production and exports of primary products of developing countries.' But, precisely because they have greatly expanded their exports of primary commodities, the prices of these exports have been increasing less fast than the prices of the manufactured goods which they import; what are called their 'terms of trade' have thus over long periods been declining. Underdeveloped countries compete for limited markets for products such as tea, coffee, sugar and rubber, and they have been unable to control the prices paid for them. A notable exception has been oil, whose producers were able to organise in OPEC (Organization of Petroleum Exporting Countries) and increase the price paid to them sixfold between 1972 and 1974. Some other attempts have been made to organise producers' cartels, for example in bananas, cocoa and bauxite, but they have not been very successful.

In general the cash crops of underdeveloped countries have been, as was said of groundnuts in Senegal, 'false riches'. Countries have had to produce more and more of them to get the same amount of goods in return. In 1960 the earnings from 25 tons of natural rubber exports from Sri Lanka would buy six tractors; by 1975 they would buy only two. The prices paid for bananas declined by 30 per cent between 1950 and 1970. And in their desperate search for foreign exchange, underdeveloped countries do produce more and more, thus setting up a vicious circle of over-production and declining prices. Ten years after their revolution even Cubans, whose revolutionary leaders had spoken of the servitude of sugar, found themselves resorting to the chimera of the ten-million-ton sugar harvest. The developed countries, for their part, are of course anxious to ensure that underdeveloped countries continue to be reliable suppliers of cheap raw materials. As Clarence B. Randall, president of US Inland Steel Company and adviser on foreign aid in Washington, said in his book *The Communist Challenge to American Business*, commenting on the fortunate availability of uranium deposits in the Belgian Congo:

What a break it was for us that the mother country was on our side! And who can possibly foresee today which of the vast unexplored areas of the world may likewise possess some unique deposit of a rare raw material which in the fullness of time our industry or our defense program may most urgently need?

Underdeveloped countries, producing mainly primary commodities and raw materials for the developed countries, Have three more problems: the prices for their primary commodities and raw materials not only decline in relative and sometimes in absolute terms, but they fluctuate widely from year to year; their economies are highly dependent on exports; and many of them are also dependent on the export of a few, sometimes one or two, commodities.

The fluctuations in commodity prices can be dramatic. They are accentuated by speculation on commodity markets, many of them in London, which are of course outside the control of the underdeveloped countries. In the mid-1970s, the price paid for sugar dropped from 64 cents a pound to 6 cents a pound in 18 months. Tanzania's first five-year plan was based on a minimum world sisal price of £90; soon afterwards, the price dropped to £60. In the late fifties, cocoa prices went in US$ from $1,000 per ton one year to $400 the next, then back to $1,000, then down to less than $600. In his 1972 speech to the United Nations, President Salvador Allende of Chile said that over the previous 12 months the decline in prices for copper had meant 'a loss of about $200 million in income for a nation whose exports total a bit more than $1,000 million', while some imports cost as much as 60 per cent more. The Brandt Report, referring to Zambia, says that a boom in copper prices took the price to $3,034 in April 1974; it then fell to $1,290 before the end of the year:

> But the prices of imports continued to rise so that the volume of imports Zambia could buy fell by 45 per cent between 1974 and 1975 and the GDP fell by 15 per cent. The gravity of this situation is put in perspective when it is contrasted with the 'oil shock' of 1974. This resulted in an increased oil bill for the industrialised countries equivalent to about 2.5 per cent of their GNP.

Underdeveloped countries are not only subjected to the 'impersonal' fluctuations of commodity markets; they are subject to the whims of their clients who may make their decisions on where to buy on political as well as on economic grounds. Susan George, in *Feeding the Few: Corporate Control of Food*, gives some, admittedly extreme, examples of the effects this can have: between 1975 and 1976, according to US Department of Agriculture statistics, the value of Brazil's sugar exports to the United States dropped from $100 million to zero; the Philippines' exports of sugar increased threefold; Guinea's cocoa exports to the United States fell from nearly two million pounds to nothing; Mexico's cotton exports to the United States were halved, while India's increased by 400 per cent and Pakistan's dropped by 90 per cent; and so on.

When underdeveloped countries are confronted with such situations, they either have to cut their consumption further still or, if they can, they borrow, which only makes their foreign exchange problems worse in the future. The fluctuations would not matter so much if the economies of underdeveloped countries had not been made highly dependent on exports of primary commodities. Their self-sufficiency was largely destroyed during the colonial period, and they are dependent on exports to pay for imports of manufactured goods and also, as has been said, of food. Exports of primary commodities and raw materials, according to the World Bank's 1980 *World Development Report*, amounted to 81 per cent of the total exports of the 'low income countries'. According to the Brandt Report, moreover, in the early seventies more than half the developing countries, excluding the oil-exporting countries, got more than half of their export earnings from only one or two commodities. Zambia got 94 per cent from copper, Mauritius 90 per cent from sugar, Cuba 84 per cent from sugar, Gambia 85 per cent from groundnuts and groundnut oil. And so on.

Some countries have escaped from this historically imposed division of labour, and others may yet do so. The United States started its process of industrialisation towards the end of the nineteenth century, through a deliberate policy of protection; as Alexander Hamilton, the first Secretary of the Treasury of the United States, said in his *Report on Manufactures* in 1891:

The United States cannot exchange with Europe on equal terms; and the want of reciprocity would render them the victim of a system which should induce them to confine their views to Agriculture, and refrain from Manufactures. A constant and increasing necessity, on their part, for the commodities of Europe, and only a partial and occasional demand for their own, in return, could not but expose them to a state of impoverishment, compared to the opulence to which their political and natural advantages authorise them to aspire.

Japan, whose markets had been opened up to imports from Europe by force in 1854 when Commander Perry sailed into Tokyo harbour, later succeeded in prohibiting foreign investments. This self-imposed isolation, which lasted until quite recently, produced, as is well known, remarkable results. The Japanese did not get foreign car companies to make their cars in Japan; they started making their own from scratch not much more than 20 years ago. At first they barely worked but now, of course, they have a big and increasing share of the developed countries' markets.

Since the 1960s the governments of underdeveloped countries have themselves been pressing for better treatment in their trade with developed countries. The first United Nations Conference on Trade and Development met in 1964, with Raul Prebisch as its Secretary-General, and was based largely on his theories on the declining terms of trade. The demands put forward were for 'fair and remunerative' prices for primary commodity exports, stabilisation of their prices, better access to the markets of industrialised countries for manufactured products, and more financial aid. Later, in the 1970s, the representatives of underdeveloped countries put forward the idea of a New International Economic Order, whose proposals were basically similar and included demands for greater international justice. But such appeals to the better feelings of the governments of developed countries have met with little response. There are some signs that the latter may be prepared to make some progress on commodity agreements, presumably because more stable prices are potentially in the interest of most people concerned (apart from those who make their livelihood from speculation) and also because there is currently some concern about the availability of certain raw materials. But the possessors of privileges, especially if they are governments or private companies, do not usually give them away except under pressure, and the only really effective pressure exercised so far in this field has been that of OPEC. In any case it is rather hard to see what 'fair and remunerative prices' might be, or indeed who exactly would benefit from them, other than the elites who are demanding them. For peasants in underdeveloped countries receive only a small fraction of the world market price for their products, however low that may be.

Exports of Capital

Cecil Rhodes, who himself made a large fortune from gold and diamonds in Southern Africa, wrote in 1896:

> I was in the East End ... and attended a meeting of the unemployed. I listened to the wild speeches, which were just a cry for 'bread', 'bread', 'bread', and on my way home I pondered over the scene and I became more than ever convinced of the importance of imperialism ... My cherished idea is a solution for the social problem, i.e. in order to save the 40,000,000 inhabitants of the United Kingdom from a bloody civil war, we, colonial statesmen, must acquire new lands to settle the surplus population, to provide new markets for the goods produced by them in the factories and mines. The Empire, as I have always said, is a bread and butter question.

The growth of imperialism towards the end of the nineteenth century was clearly seen, at least by some of its protagonists, as a solution to the economic problems of, for example, Britain.

Palme Dutt in his book written in the 1950s, *The Crisis of Britain and the British Empire*, comments:

> The imperialist economy of Britain is a parasitic economy. It is increasingly dependent on world tribute for its maintenance. By the eve of the first world war close on two-fifths of British imports were no longer paid for by

exports of goods; and this proportion had risen still higher by the eve of the second world war ... By 1951 [the imports surplus] had soared to a total of £779 million.

British deficits in 'visible' trade, or goods, are still these days partly covered by surpluses in 'invisibles', in other words in payments for shipping and insurance, and also repatriated profits and interest payments from overseas investments and loans.

Marx had argued that, as the mechanisation of industry proceeded in response to competitive pressures, rates of profit would decline and the survival of capitalism would be threatened. Lenin, writing on *Imperialism: the Highest Stage of Capitalism* in 1916, argued that capitalism had been able to give itself a new lease of life and counteract the tendency for profits to decline by investing 'surplus capital' overseas in order to take advantage of lower wages and cheap land and raw materials. Such capital was of course not surplus to social needs; it was surplus only in the sense that it was difficult to find uses for it profitable to its owners.

The question that is currently exercising the financial authorities of the West, that of 'recyclying' petrodollars (i.e. the money invested in Western banks by the governments of oil-producing countries) can only be understood as a 'problem' in terms of the banks' difficulty in finding somewhere to invest the money which will be both profitable to themselves and safe. The recession in the industrialised countries has reduced the possibilities for the money to be invested there. In the early 1970s the banks therefore lent on a massive scale to the governments of underdeveloped countries; they are now considered to be dangerously overextended. The debt problem of some underdeveloped countries is assuming crisis proportions. This is why the Brandt Report, for example, is arguing the need for international 'pump-priming' — re-starting the process of growth in developed countries by lending money to underdeveloped countries for them to buy the products of the West — and why a need is also seen to strengthen international institutions such as the World Bank and the International Monetary Fund which can regulate the necessary lending and ensure that there are no defaults.

Whatever is thought of the 'capital surplus' theory, there are other possible explanations for the big increase in loans and investments abroad which took place at the end of the nineteenth century. One is that, with the growth of other industrialised powers in Europe, British capitalists in particular felt the need to invest abroad in order to protect their markets and sources of raw materials. In addition, loans were made for the improvement of transport facilities for the extraction of these materials; the loans were spent on the purchase of rails, rolling stock, and so on in Britain, and thus also served the purpose of enlarging the markets for British industry. In Lenin's words, 'the export of capital thus becomes a means for encouraging the export of commodities.' The process of extracting the materials needed for British industry, in particular metals, became more complicated and more investment was therefore necessary. More important perhaps, industry was becoming concentrated into increasingly larger units, or monopolies; capitalism was growing by a process of large firms absorbing small ones. As competition between small firms was eliminated and moved to a new level it became not only possible, but increasingly necessary for the security of the large monopolies, that they should control their markets and sources of supply and also that they should be able to expand into wider and wider areas.

The process of concentration overseas began with small trading companies uniting into notorious conglomerates such as the United Africa Company, the Compagnie Francaise d'Afrique Occidentale and the United Fruit Company. These were companies that secured raw materials and agricultural products from the dependent areas. They subsequently diversified into manufacturing in the metropolis, shipping, transport; or they became subsidiaries of manufacturing concerns in the metropolis. The United Africa Company, itself a product of mergers in Africa organised by Lever Bros., started by making soap in Liverpool, became a subsidiary of Unilever when this Anglo-Dutch monopoly combine was formed in 1929, and ensured that its factories in Europe were kept supplied with palm oil and the other oils needed for the manufacture of soap and margarine. Other monopolies or oligopolies grew up by similar processes and were the forerunners of what are now known as multinationals or transnational or global firms, which merely means firms owning assets in more than one country.

Multinational companies today control between a quarter and a third of all world production. The total sales of their foreign affiliates in 1976, according to the Brandt Report, were estimated at $830 billion 'which is about the same as the then gross national product of all developing countries', excluding the ones that export oil, and which is also more than the total value of all direct exports from developed countries. 'In addition to oil,' the Brandt Report adds, 'the marketing, processing or production of several commodities — including bauxite, copper, iron ore, nickel, lead, zinc, tin, tobacco, bananas and tea — is dominated in each case by a small number of transnational corporations.'

Although there is some disagreement about this, it appears that the profits made abroad were generally considerably higher than the profits made in the metropolis. Even if they had not been, they could still have ensured that the average rate of profit for all industries was higher than it would otherwise have been. But Mandel, for example, explaining that 'colonial super-profits' were possible because of the 'super-exploitation' of labour, gives a number of examples of American, British and Belgian firms making very much higher profits abroad than in their respective countries of origin. Writers in the 'white man's burden' tradition have argued that investments overseas by capitalist firms based in Europe, and later the United States, have 'developed' the rest of the world. Even if the profits were at times rather high, it is said, this was the price that had to be paid for receiving the initial investment and for the risks involved. It is not usually denied that the return flows — in the form of repatriated profits, dividends, patent fees, management fees, salaries to foreign technicians and consultants and so on — have much exceeded the original investments. But it is maintained that this is the normal price that has to be paid for getting the investment in the first place: naturally the capital, or loan, has to be repaid with profit or interest.

This ignores two important general points: first, that the investments are not the ones that would have been made if the concern had been the welfare of the inhabitants of under-

developed countries rather than the profits of foreign
capitalists; and second, that, since much of the capital is in fact
raised in underdeveloped countries and is foreign only in
ownership and control, if it were owned and controlled by the
peoples of the underdeveloped countries the profits could
potentially be used for the improvement of their standard of
living rather than that of the foreign owners. There is also
evidence that the return flows on capital invested in
underdeveloped countries are higher than the return flows
resulting from investments in Europe and thus might be considered 'abnormal'. For example, in 1960 the capital flows
from the United States to Europe exceeded the return flows by
$500 million, whereas for the underdeveloped countries the
reverse was the case: the latter exceeded the former by $1,100
million. And, according to *US News and World Report*, in the
five years 1956-61 there was a ratio of inflow to the United
States to outflow from the United States of 147 per cent for
Latin America, 164 per cent for the underdeveloped countries
as a whole, and 43 per cent for Western Europe. This tends to
vitiate the argument that the return flows from underdeveloped
countries are 'normal' and 'natural', rather than the result of
any form of super-exploitation or super-profits.

It can in fact be argued that investments overseas by the
metropolitan powers have constituted a new means of draining
wealth out of the underdeveloped countries. Gunder Frank, in
Dependent Accumulation and Underdevelopment, makes the
point in the case of India:

> Two of the principal instruments the British used to drain
> India of its capital were the railroads and the debt. The
> railroads were not only the physical instruments used to
> restructure the economy in order to be able to suck raw
> materials out and pump manufactured commodities in
> along the right of way. The Indians were also obliged to
> pay themselves for the installation of this exploitative
> mechanism on their soil. And the 'Indian debt', to which
> all imaginable and unimaginable items of British colonial
> adminstration were charged, became in the particular cir-
> cumstances of India one of the principal fiscal instruments
> for extracting the economic surplus from the colony to the
> metropolis.

In most of the major Latin American countries, the first railways were built with domestic capital which also opened up the copper and nitrate mines in Chile. It was only after these became booming businesses that they were taken over by foreigners; similarly, these days, much of foreign 'investment' is actually the take-over of existing local businesses. But says Gunder Frank:

> The railway network and electric grid, far from being net- or grid-like, was ray-like and connected the hinterland of each country and sometimes of several countries with the port of entry and exit, which was in turn connected with the metropolis.

The same can be said of nearly all of the investments in the so-called economic infrastructure which were financed then and which continue to be financed by agencies such as the World Bank: they serve the purpose of facilitating the extraction of the country's raw materials for consumption in Europe and the United States, and the operation of foreign business in general. Moreover, they are eventually paid for by the peoples of the underdeveloped countries themselves.

It is part of the mythology of the accepted orthodoxy that the West is now 'helping' underdeveloped countries, through official aid and private investment, to escape from their poverty. It is amazing that this can be so. Quite apart from the historical effects of plunder and distortion, quite apart from any of the injustices of existing forms of trade, there are quantifiable and quite easily discernible outflows of money from underdeveloped to developed countries which, increasingly, exceed any new inflows. The debt of underdeveloped countries has now reached staggering proportions; according to the World Bank's 1980 *World Development Report*, 'low-income oil-importing developing countries' had in 1977 to spend 10.1 per cent of their export proceeds on servicing their foreign debt and 'middle-income oil-importing countries' had to spend 19.8 per cent. If repatriated profits on foreign investment, interest payments, royalty payments, debt repayments, private capital sent abroad and so on, are added up, they exceed capital inflows in the form of official aid and private loans and investments. The fact that most underdeveloped countries have deficits on their current accounts is rather misleading, since the figures on current accounts include, for example, repatriated profits and interest payments. Thus some underdeveloped countries, in order to pay for these outflows, must currently export more *goods* to the developed countries than they receive from them, even at the prevailing prices; according to the Brandt Report, exports of goods from underdeveloped countries to developed countries amount to $216 billion, whereas they receive from them only $200 billion of goods at current prices.

A large part of the money outflows from underdeveloped countries is accounted for by the repatriated profits of foreign-owned business. Richard J. Barnet and Ronald E. Muller, in their book *Global Reach*, describe this as a system of 'welfare in reverse', and say that, 'incredible as it may seem, the poor countries have been an indispensable source of finance capital for the worldwide expansion of global corporations.' Foreign companies investing in underdeveloped countries probably raise, on average, around 80 per cent of their capital in the underdeveloped countries themselves. They are able to do so because individual investors and banks, many of them foreign-owned but relying on deposits by local people, prefer to put their money in large multinational companies rather than in more risky local enterprises. Multinational companies are now also anxious to arrange local participation and joint ventures for political reasons. Moreover the amounts which are brought in from abroad are generally exaggerated in official figures. *Business Abroad*, an American business publication, describes the overseas investment practises of US corporations thus:

> In calculating the value of capital investment, General Motors, for example, figures the intangibles such as trademarks, patents, and know-how equivalent to twice the actual invested capital. Some corporations calculate know-how, blueprints, and so on as one-third of capital investment, and then supply one-third in equity by providing machinery and equipment.

And yet the profits go to the metropolis. Barnet and Muller say:

> Between 1965 and 1968, 52 per cent of all profits of United

States subsidiaries operating in Latin America in manufacturing ... were repatriated to the United States ... even
though 78 per cent of the investment funds used to
generate that dollar of profit came from local sources. If
we look at the mining, petroleum and smelting industries,
the capital outflow resulting from the operations of global
corporations is even worse. Each dollar of profit is based
on an investment that was 83 per cent financed from local
savings; yet only 21 per cent of the profit remains in the
local economy ... A retired executive of one of the three
largest multinational banks recalls for us that in the late
1950s and early 1960s his bank always tried to use about 95
per cent local savings sources for its local loans and no
more than five per cent of its dollar holdings.

A US Department of Commerce report (1979D) gives the
percentage of new funds from the United States in total investment in less-developed countries in 1972-74 as *minus* 28 per
cent. Moreover, in many cases the 'investments' made are not
investments in new undertakings but are simply takeovers of
existing, locally owned enterprises. Barnet and Muller report
that:

Of the 717 new manufacturing subsidiaries established in
Latin America (between 1958 and 1967) by the top 187 US-
based global corporations ... 46 per cent were established
by buying out of existing local firms.

Such activity can hardly be described as new 'development'.
   The profits themselves are extremely high; it is said to be
normal for investments to pay for themselves in three to five
years, and some companies investing in underdeveloped countries state openly that they expect to get their money back in
one or two years. 'I should not really tell you this,' a vice-
president of a US-based global bank confided to Barnet and
Muller, 'but while we earn around 13 to 14 per cent on our
United States operations, we can easily count on a 33 per cent
rate of return on our business conducted in Latin America.'
This confession may have been somewhat disingenuous,
because there is quite a bit of evidence to show that profits are
a good deal higher even than this. Accounting is an art rather

than a science, and companies report different levels of profits
to different agencies: low ones to the governments to whom
they must pay taxes and high ones to potential investors.

Multinational companies make extensive use of the system
of 'transfer prices'. Since more than half of United States exports takes the form of exports from US parent companies to
their subsidiaries and over 30 per cent of all world trade consists of transactions within multinational companies, such
companies can avoid duties and taxes by valuing the goods
traded at levels different from world market prices according
to where they want to show a profit. Thus a good deal of no-
tional buying and selling takes place in 'tax havens'. Goods can
be shipped, for example, from the United Stats to the Bahamas
and then 're-exported' to their destination in Latin America at
a much higher price; the 'profits' are made in the Bahamas,
where there is no taxation. To get a true picture of profits from
a subsidiary, Barnet and Muller say:

> it is necessary to include in the calculation overpricing of
> imports and underpricing of exports as well as reported
> profits, royalties and fees repatriated to the global head-
> quarters. This total can then be divided into the declared
> net worth of the subsidiary. Vaitsos (in a 1972 Harvard D.
> Phil thesis) performed this exercise for 15 wholly-owned
> drug subsidiaries of United States and European-based
> global corporations. He found the effective annual rate of
> return ranged from a low of 38.1 per cent to a high of
> 962.1 per cent with an average of 79.1 per cent. Yet that
> year these firms' average declared profits submitted to the
> Colombian tax authorities was 6.7 per cent. In the rubber
> industry the effective profit rate on the average was 43 per
> cent; the declared profit rate, 16 per cent ... But even
> these estimates understate the actual profits being
> generated. For example, [they could not] take account of
> the underpricing of exports or the fact that the subsidiary's
> net worth is usually considerably overvalued.

An assistant to the president of a large United States based
global corporation operating in Latin America told Barnet and
Muller it was 'no problem' to maintain real rates of return
from 50 per cent to 400 per cent a year.

It is sometimes said that these outflows are the price that underdeveloped countries have to pay for receiving the technology which only the multinational companies have access to. It is certainly true that multinational companies have the resources to engage in research on a scale that nobody else does, and that their control of certain advanced forms of technology partly accounts for their oligopolistic power. They hang on to this control as much as they can and transfer as little as they can of the technology. In addition, they transfer technology in such a way that the subsidiary in the underdeveloped country is tied to purchases from the parent company, which often implies additional costs. When their investments in underdeveloped countries are merely the taking over of existing enterprises, they clearly do not supply any new technology. But when they do make new investments, some of their technology is necessarily spread. The question is whether it's enough and of the right sort to make the sacrifices involved in getting it, for the majority at least, worthwhile. Since the bargaining power of underdeveloped countries is weak, the transferred technology is often over-priced and/or obsolete. In addition (as is so often said that it has become a cliché) the technology introduced into underdeveloped countries is not necessarily the most appropriate technology; it has been developed to be marketed in advanced industrialised societies with different patterns of consumption and income levels. In any case, the concern of private companies is to make profits out of a given distribution of income rather than to eliminate the poverty and hardship that exists in developed as well as underdeveloped societies. The following example from Baran shows the sort of considerations that sometimes influence research:

> When du Pont developed a pigment which could be utilised either in paints or as a textile dye, the director of one of its research laboratories wrote: 'further work may be necessary on adding contaminants to Monastral colours to make them unsatisfactory on textiles but satisfactory for paints.'

One of the most important problems with imported technology is that very often it eliminates more jobs than it creates. This is now a problem throughout the world, but it is more severe in underdeveloped countries where unemployment, even according to inadequate official statistics, is already very high. There are innumerable examples; here is one from the *Wall Street Journal*:

> Far from helping such workers ... Brazil's modernisation actually victimises thousands. When a salt company bought new equipment, efficiency soared — but 7000 people lost their jobs. In Ponce de Varvalhos, many suffer indirectly from the modernisation of sugar plantations in far off parts of Brazil. This has made the local plantations uneconomic ... A 60-year-old woman who had worked 20 years on one plantation says she and 1000 other workers were told to 'harvest your crop, plant grass for cattle, and get out'. She now earns $6.50 a month washing clothes. A 41-year-old man who worked 18 years at the Mary-of-Mercy sugar mill now peddles bread by the roadside for 54 cents a day.

In a rational planned system, improvements in efficiency could lead to higher incomes for everybody, more leisure, or more investment elsewhere. But in a capitalist underdeveloped country they tend merely to add to the army of unemployed and malnourished.

Perhaps even more important than the multinationals' control of technology is their control of marketing techniques. Galbraith has said that the real planners are multinational corporations; they decide what consumers are to eat, drink and wear, what they will have in their houses, and what they will pay for it. The head of a multinational food company spoke as follows:

> How often we see in developing countries that the poorer the economic outlook the more important the small luxury of a flavoured soft drink or smoke ... to the dismay of many would-be benefactors the poorer the malnourished are, the more likely they are to spend a disproportionate amount of whatever they have on some luxury rather than on what they need ... Observe, study, learn. We try to do it. It seems to pay off for us. Perhaps it will for you too.

Such is the stength of the ideology of dependency that imported products are often preferred to local products, even when they are similar or actually inferior and more expensive. People's diets are deteriorating as white bread, for example, is substituted for more nutritional local foods, and as the consumption of soft drinks grows. Albert Stridsberg notes with satisfaction (in *Advertising Age*, 22 September 1969) that the popularity of Coca-Cola, for example, is due to the advertising campaigns of the transnationals and that:

> It has long been known that in the poorest regions of Mexico, where soft drinks play a functional role in the diet, it is the international brands — Coke and Pepsi — not local brands, which dominate. Likewise, a Palestinian refugee urchin, shining shoes in Beirut, saves his piastres for a real Coca-Cola, at twice the price of a local cola.

Up to 1966, the British Institute of Marketing's definition of marketing was: 'assessing consumer needs'. Then it changed to: 'assessing and converting customer purchase power into effective demand for a specific product ... so as to achieve the profit target or other objectives set by a company'.

Aid

About one-third of the flows of capital to underdeveloped countries consists of what is known as official aid, or loans and grants from governments and international agencies; the other two-thirds is private, mainly private bank loans (now between a third and a half of the total), direct private investment, and private export credits. Most of the official 'aid' provided is in the form of loans, usually at relatively low rates of interest, for specific projects; the money is usually 'tied': in other words it must be spent on the goods of the country providing it. The 'aid' amounts provided have been declining in relation to the national incomes of the providing countries. The average percentage for the developed countries of the West in 1978 was 0.35 per cent; the British percentage was 0.48 per cent; the percentage for the Arab OPEC countries was 2.55 per cent. Some of the money is channelled through 'multilateral' organisations such as the World Bank, the IMF (International Monetary Fund) and United Nations agencies like the FAO (Food & Agriculture Organisation).

The main growth of official government aid has taken place since the second world war. It can be seen as a means of maintaining, especially after the loss of colonies, a common interest between the elites of underdeveloped countries and the metropolitan countries, or as a kind of bribe to help to make it worth their while to continue to co-operate with the drain of capital from their countries. A common ideology of 'development' grew up, and the purpose of aid is supposed to be to promote 'development'. Some of the projects financed by aid have been obviously useful; and some of those administering aid no doubt genuinely believe that its main purpose is to eliminate poverty. But the development promoted through aid is of a particular variety: as before, it is development (if at all) strictly in accordance with the interests of the metropolitan powers and with the interests of their capitalists in particular. As a memorandum from the Confederation of British Industry to the House of Commons Select Committee on Overseas Aid put it in 1969: 'for British industry, help to the Third World is in a sense an investment in the development of markets and sources of supply for raw materials.' The former president of the World Bank, Mr Eugene Black, drumming up support for aid in the 1950s, said:

> Our foreign aid programs constitute a distinct benefit to American business. The three major benefits are: (1) foreign aid provides a substantial and immediate market for United States goods and services. (2) foreign aid stimulates the development of new overseas markets for United States companies. (3) foreign aid orients national economies toward a free enterprise system in which United States firms can prosper.

President Kennedy's view is well known: 'Foreign aid,' he said in 1961, 'is a method by which the United States maintains a position of influence and control around the world and sustains a good many countries which would definitely collapse or pass into the Communist bloc.' President Nixon, in his 1968 presidential campaign, was a bit less elegant: 'let us remember that the main purpose of American aid is not to help other nations but to help ourselves.'

Aid 'helps' those who provide it in a number of direct and indirect ways. Since 'bilateral' aid is nearly always tied, it can be used not only to open up new markets but also to sell otherwise uncompetitive products. It has been estimated that the average price of goods financed by aid is 25 per cent above world market prices. Since aid is usually provided in the form of loans and, moreover, is usually only available for the direct foreign exchange costs of projects, it commits governments to spending their own resources in ways that are considered helpful. In particular, it causes governments to spend money on the 'economic infrastructure', especially transport, communications and power, which is necessary for the profitable operation of foreign business. It also makes governments dependent on more loans to repay their past loans and, therefore, presumably more compliant. Above all, it is used to support 'friendly' governments and friendly people within those governments. Right-wing regimes are the main recipients of aid. Left-wing or even merely progressive regimes commonly have aid to them reduced or altogether cut; when they are overthrown by military coups, the new friendly regimes are rewarded with renewed largesse. When left-wing governments do receive aid, the amounts involved are often token; they can also be explained as part of an attempt to win them away from left-wing policies.

Within governments, aid agencies identify 'our men' and back them with aid. Sometimes 'our men' in government are actually the nationals of the aid agency concerned. For example Professor Bell, a United States citizen, was on the staff of the Pakistan Planning Board in the 1950s; he testified to the United States Senate Foreign Relations Committee:

> After a while, when the Planning Board began to have reasonable views as to what sort of things made sense to be done and what sort of things did not make sense — the [US] Mission began to use this information to guide them in making their own decisions as to what they wanted to put their money into.

In South Korea, the most important government agency

responsible for economic policy is the Korean Development Institute (KDI); representatives of the World Bank and the IMF are on its staff. Professor Cummings, of the University of Washington, comments:

> Korea today, unlike in the 1950s, has the economy that the major market economies want it to have; this should be no surprise, since countries like the United States, Japan and West Germany, and organisations like the World Bank and the International Monetary Fund have participated in planning South Korean development.

The central bank and economic ministries of Zaire are virtually run by officials of the World Bank and the IMF. In Brazil in 1964, after the populist government of Goulart was overthrown by a military coup, 'our man in Brazil' was above all Roberto Campos — Minister of Finance, former ambassador to Washington, one of the eminent persons consulted by the Brandt Commission, and now Brazilian ambassador in London — otherwise known as Bobby Fields. In Thailand, the aid agencies apparently have good relations with Boonchu Rojanasathien, Deputy Premier for Economic Affairs, who began a speech thus: 'We used to talk of Japan Inc. and of Singapore Inc. Ladies and gentlemen, I would like to announce the arrival of Thailand Inc. This concept, I believe, sums up all that I wish to say this morning.'

Aid is of course not always used as a means of promoting particular economic policies, over which economists and others devoted more or less disinterestedly to the goal of development may genuinely disagree. Often it is used merely as a political weapon. At times it is used with brutal cynicism and can be especially so in the important case of food aid. Quite a large number of underdeveloped countries have allowed themselves to become heavily dependent on this form of aid, especially the variety supplied by the United States in what are known as 'Food for Peace' programmes. Food aid has been much criticised for providing a disincentive to agricultural programmes for greater self-sufficiency. It is also highly susceptible to political manipulation. Dan Ellerman, of the US National Security Council, said in 1974: 'to give food aid to countries just because people are starving is a pretty weak reason.' But there are other reasons, as the Office of Political Research of the Central Intelligence Agency points out:

> In a cooler and therefore hungrier world, the United States near-monopoly as a food-exporter ... could give the United States a measure of power it never had before — possibly an economic and political dominance greater than that of the immediate post-World War II ... years ... Washington could acquire virtual life and death power over the fate of multitudes of the needy.

As Earl Butz, then United States Secretary of Agriculture, said at the 1974 World Food Conference in Rome, food 'is one of the principal tools in our negotiating kit'. And Senator Hubert Humphrey, later Vice-President, with a certain reputation for liberalism, said in 1957:

> I have heard ... that people may become dependent on us for food. I know that was not supposed to be good news. To me, that was good news, because before people can do anything they have got to eat. And if you are looking for a way to get people to lean on you and be dependent on you, in terms of their co-operation with you, it seems to me that food dependence would be terrific.

An example of how this can work out in practise is given in the Indian periodical *Economic and Political Weekly*, in an article by Rehman Sobhan called 'Politics of Food and Famine in Bangladesh'. It describes how the United States attempted to get the somewhat leftish Bangladeshi government of Shaikh Mujib, which was 'dependent' on food imports but was not at the time very co-operative, to co-operate. In 1974 between 27,000 and 100,000 Bangladeshi died in what the article says was mainly a 'manmade' famine. There were the worst floods for several decades. Blame was laid on hoarding and speculation by grain producers and traders and on the conservatism of the food ministry. But the 'primal source of the crisis lay in the breakdown of the import programme ... The United States appears to have opted for a dramatic demonstration of the awesome power of food politics.' In the early part of 1973, the United States was delaying its normal commitments of food aid, aware that the government was already having difficulties because of the rising prices of food and oil imports. The government managed to get some grain from the Soviet Union, but:

> Bangladesh's parlous external financial position was elicited by potential commercial creditors from western donor agencies themselves. As a result in the summer of 1974 two crucial grain shipments contracted with United States grain exporters were cancelled because of ... doubts over Bangladesh's creditworthiness. It is not clear whether this was encouraged by the United States government as part of its own plans to bring Bangladesh to its knees; but it is known that United States grain shippers work closely with the United States government.

The Bangladesh political leadership was 'in no mood for political heroics'; the necessary assurances were given and the government's investment policy was also revised in favour of the private sector and foreign enterprise. Even so, 'the United States continued to drive in the boot by further withholding commitments' on the grounds that Bangladesh had contracted to sell jute to Cuba.

> The crucial delay between the surrender of the Bangladesh government to United States pressure and the actual signature of the agreement happened while floods were ravaging Bangladesh ... famine victims were dying in the streets of Dacca ... This grim drama was being transacted in the full view and knowledge of the United States embassy.

The idea seems to have been to deflect Shaikh Mujib from left-wing policies. But in the end he was murdered anyway, perhaps with the connivance of the CIA, and replaced by the most pro-Western of his colleagues.

The policies promoted through 'aid' are not always so directly political nor are they necessarily directly related to the immediate interests of foreign investors. Aid is also supposed to promote economic policies favourable to 'development'. The institutions providing funds — especially the two most powerful, the World Bank and the International Monetary Fund — insist that their advice is purely technical, value-free and objective; after all, the World Bank and the IMF are international institutions. But in fact the recommendations follow a predictable pattern, which accords with an easily recognisable right-wing ideology and which has at times caused considerable hardship to the peoples of the countries receiving 'aid'. The ideological nature of the advice given is not surprising; even supposedly international institutions are dominated by the major powers that provide their funds. Both the World Bank and the IMF were set up after the second world war to solve the problems of the rich countries, which negotiated their establishment at Bretton Woods. The World Bank's statutes specifically enjoin it to promote the flow of private investment to underdeveloped countries, and an internal memorandum states that it must not lend to countries that nationalise without adequate compensation, default on their debts or act in other ways unsatisfactory to private investors.

The World Bank, the International Monetary Fund and the United States AID (Agency for International Development) in many cases work out detailed programmes which the government concerned is to adopt as a condition of getting their money. This is so well known in the case of the IMF that there have on occasions been anti-IMF riots and governments wishing to carry out an IMF programme have been forced to retract or resign. The United States AID has published accounts of its methods of 'leverage'. It is less well known in the case of the World Bank, one of whose officials professed a belief in 'secret diplomacy'. But in fact the three agencies work closely together, for example holding meetings in the United States Embassy in the country concerned to co-ordinate their demands.

The conditions they attach to their lending are sometimes precisely quantified: for example, a government must devalue by such-and-such an amount, it must cut government expenditures by so much, it must reduce its restrictions on imports by such-and-such an amount. The major purpose of the conditions can be seen to be: to ensure the smooth functioning of the system, financial stability, the avoidance of debt defaults and nationalisations, the avoidance of restrictions on the outflow of profits or restrictions on imports, the promotion of the private sector and reliance on the free play of market forces.

Governments are expected to 'adjust' to their resulting problems through austerity measures: cuts in government spending, especially for 'social' purposes, to balance the budget; cuts in wages, 'in order to reduce inflation'; restrictions on credit; increases in rents and in the prices charged for transport and other facilities.

Such policies are justified, as they currently are in Britain and in the arguments of the 'monetarist' school of thought, on the grounds that they provide the only satisfactory basis for steady growth in the future. Meanwhile they hit the poor, cutting real incomes and adding to unemployment, and the growth is elusive. André Gunder Frank gives a graphic description of the effects of the methodical application of such policies by the Pinochet regime in Chile in *Economic Genocide in Chile: Monetarist Theory versus Humanity*. Recent internal documents of the IMF expressed the view that the Pinochet regime was not cutting wages enough. In 1976, at a time when human rights pressures were beginning to make it difficult for the United States government to continue to provide aid to the Chilean regime, the World Bank, urged on by the United States administration and by McNamara, approved two large loans to Chile. McNamara announced that other projects were in preparation but that their approval would depend on the junta's willingness to pursue 'sound economic policies' and improve creditworthiness.

This embroilment in the policies of the Pinochet regime in Chile, for example, makes it hard to believe that there have been any real changes in the policies of the major financial agencies. It is nevertheless claimed that there have been. Certainly the tone of the literature and speeches has changed. At the 1973 Annual Meeting of the World Bank in Nairobi, McNamara made a much-quoted speech in which he said that the Bank must redirect its activities towards the rural and urban poor, those whose condition of life, he said, is 'so degraded by disease, illiteracy, malnutrition and squalor as to deny its victims basic human necessities'. A flood of literature on 'basic needs' and how to supply them followed in publications of the International Labour Organisation, in a book sponsored by the World Bank called *Redistribution with Growth*, and so on. Well-meaning solutions are proposed:

basic improvements in agricultural practices, the spread of forms of education adapted to real needs, simple forms of preventive medicine, the development of practical tools and machines that can be made widely available.

Those who argued that wealth would 'trickle down' are now saying that deliberate efforts should be made to ensure that it reaches the very poor directly, in particular by increasing their capacity to produce. It is suggested that governments should make deliberate efforts to reverse the tendency towards the concentration of capital and should foster small enterprises in the so-called 'informal sector'. And McNamara, in his 1980 speech to the Board of Governors, said that governments, rather than cutting expenditure, should actually spend more money for social purposes.

It all sounds impressive. The question is what it amounts to in practice. The most obvious, visible and easily quantifiable change is that the project lending of the World Bank has shifted: a much higher proportion of its loans is now spent on agriculture, education, health, the supply of clean water and so on. The projects themselves have, however, been heavily criticised. This is particularly the case with projects in rural areas financed by the World Bank and other official Western agencies. Just because a majority of the extremely poor live in rural areas does not mean that they will benefit from projects in rural areas. In fact the poor have often actually suffered from projects of the Green Revolution type favoured by the World Bank and others: the benefits have regularly been appropriated by the better-off peasants and landowners who are then in a stronger position than before to exploit the worse-off, who have a greater interest than before in acquiring more land and who do acquire it, by methods ranging from straightforward purchase to bribes and force, thus adding to the numbers of the landless. Two Americans, Betsy Hartman and James Boyce, give an account of the arrival of a World Bank-financed tubewell in the Bangladeshi village in which they were living. On paper, this tubewell, like 2,999 others, was the property of an 'irrigation group' of 25 to 50 farmers. In reality, it was the personal property of one man: Nafis, the biggest landlord of the area. It cost about $12,000, but Nafis had paid $300 for it, mostly in bribes to local officials. It could irrigate about twice the area of Nafis's land, but since the rates he charged for the water from it were high, few were interested in it, and 'he already has his eye on the plots nearest his tubewell.' A foreign expert working on the project told Hartman and Boyce: 'I no longer ask who is getting the well. I know what the answer will be, and I don't want to hear it. One-hundred per cent of these tubewells are going to the big boys.'

The phenomenon is a general one. As Harry Magdoff points out in his book *Imperialism: From the Colonial Age to the Present*:

> The obstacles [to the needed changes] are located in the social institutions under which the people live, in the type/ of landowning, in the vested interests of the large land- owners and businessmen, and in the social priorities imposed by the ruling classes. Let me cite a simple illustra- tion. One of the puzzling aspects of India's economic trials has been the seeming indifference of small farmers to undertake simple work needed to irrigate the land they work. The Indian government spends large sums of money to dig broad canals in order to make more water available for farming. But the farmers failed to take advantage of this potential boost to their output; they did not dig the ditches needed to bring the water from the rivers and canals to their small plots. I once asked a leading United States agricultural specialist who had spent a great deal of time in India: What went wrong? Was it laziness? Stupidi- ty? Ignorance? The conservative agronomist laughed at my naive questions. The simplest and most ignorant farmer, he explained patiently, knows the importance of water. But the irrigation ditches had to pass over land owned by big landowners who exacted a tax for the use of the ditches — a tax the farmers could not possibly pay.

The World Bank and other foreign experts can and do say that this is not their fault, and of course they are partly right. 'We all have yet to discover,' notes Mahbub ul Haq, a promi- nent Pakistani economist and an official of the World Bank, 'how alternative delivery systems can be devised to reach the poor people and obtain their willing and enthusiastic co- operation.' Another Bank official claims, 'Bank-financed programmes for rural credits have been deliberately reoriented to make sure that an increasing proportion of credits accrue to disadvantaged groups who formerly had no access to institutional credit.' But their protestations would be more convincing if it were possible to demonstrate that they favoured governments with radical egalitarian policies; in fact, it is easier to demonstrate the opposite. It is clear in any case that the Bank's ideological position favours the creation of a stable and conservative class of small producers. To the extent that it supports land reform at all, it favours the distribution of land to individual peasants in not-too-small units; it certainly does not support the collective ownership of the means of production, in particular of land. And yet, as Hartman and Boyce point out, if land were to be redistributed to individuals in Bangladesh, the resulting plots would be far too small to provide adequate susbsistence for all the existing landless people in Bangladesh. The same is true of many other countries where 'mini-plots' are already a major source of hardship. The following is probably a fairly typical Bank reaction: in response to some Dutch critics of the distributional aspects of a Bank project at Funtua in Nigeria, a Bank official wrote:

> A project on [this] scale would not take off at all unless we had the support [of the local hierarchy]. This in turn means working through the system rather than outside it. I am not sure whether your ... approach would work on a larger scale, purely because those in power would resent their loss of patronage. It is not our job to start social revolutions.

It is, in fact, their job to prevent them.

It is also clear that, however good or bad individual projects may be, they can never do very much, given the limited size of 'aid', without changes in central government policies. Although the Bank does not consider it its business to start social revolutions, it is certainly still in the business of influencing government policies. The World Bank has recently set up a new form of lending, called Structural Adjustment Loans; like IMF standby agreements and the Programme Loans of the United States AID (Agency for International Development), these can be directly related to the carrying out of a specific programme or set of economic policies by the government receiving the money.

The World Bank and the IMF have been called the police of development. Other official and private lenders tend to lend or not to lend according to whether the government has the 'the seal of approval' of the IMF or the World Bank. Especially now that private banks have become over-extended and fearful of defaults, these two institutions are being called upon to make sure that the banks get their money back and that they can lend in future without fear of losing it. The World Bank and the IMF are said to work together in complete harmony; no conflicts are admitted between them; and they frequently go on joint missions to countries. Although the IMF has been criticised, even in the Brandt Report, for example, for excessive 'harshness' in the conditions it puts on its lending, and may possibly have responded a little to these criticisms, it certainly has not changed a great deal. The implication is that the World Bank has not done so either and that the governments of underdeveloped countries are still subject to pressures from these institutions to carry out orthodox monetarist policies. 'In brief,' said the World Bank sternly on page (i) of its 1979 confidential report on Pakistan, 'Pakistan has been living beyond its means.' 'In summary,' the Bank said again on page 6 of the same report, 'Pakistan has been living beyond its means.' The cuts proposed were in public, rather than private, expenditures. President Nyerere has had similar experiences: 'Cuts may have to be made in our national expenditure,' he declared to a meeting on the IMF at Arusha in 1980, 'but we will decide whether they fall on public services or private expenditure.'

It is claimed that the World Bank has been pressing the government of Brazil to redistribute from its 'miracle', though now not so miracle, growth. Brazil is one of the biggest recipients of World Bank loans, but its record on income distribution is one of the most notoriously bad. Between 1960 and 1977, according to Brazilian official sources, the share of national income of the poorest half of the population fell from 17 per cent to 13 per cent, while the share of the richest one per cent rose from 12 per cent to 18 per cent, or more than the poorest half receive. It is also said that the World Bank was asking for more resources to be devoted to agriculture, which is not, in itself, necessarily a redistributive measure. There is, in general, more emphasis than before on the desirability of measures to eliminate poverty, on redistribution, on education, health, agriculture, and social questions in general. But it is doubtful whether, at central government level, this amounts to much more than exhortation, at best. Aid to Brazil, for example, will not be cut if the Brazilian government continues to fail to do anything about redistributing income. But if it were to adopt socialist measures or default on its debts, that would be a different matter altogether.

There is a feeling of *déjà vu* in the current interest in reforms among Western governments and development experts. In the 1960s, just after the Cuban revolution, the United States promoted with fanfares a programme of progressive measures, including land reform, in the so-called Alliance for Progress. (With fewer fanfares, President Carter, after the revolution in Nicaragua, began to press for reforms in neighbouring El Salvador.) 'Those who possess wealth and power in poor nations,' said President Kennedy on the first anniversary of the Alliance for Progress, 'must accept their own responsibilities. They must lead the fight for those basic reforms which alone can preserve the fabric of their own societies. Those who make peaceful revolution impossible will make violent revolution inevitable.' As the United States trade unionist Sidney Lens commented in 1963:

> We have been pushing for a 'revolution' from the 'top-down' rather than from the 'bottom-up'. We have been asking the oligarchs to sign their own death-warrants by agreeing to land reform, tax reform, and other innovations that will depress their own status. They have replied to our proddings by ruse and fraud.

When they replied, as in Honduras in 1962, by attempting to nationalise the land of the United Fruit Company, the United States government demanded that they should be paid, not in bonds, but, in the words of the supposedly liberal Senator Wayne Morse, 'in hard, cold American dollars.' Similarly, when the Colombian government in the 1960s tried to apply its rather timid land reform law to the unutilised land of a North

American timber company, United States AID threatened to cut aid.

'The Kennedy Administration gave diplomatic recognition to all seven of the military coups which took place during its existence,' notes Horowitz, 'despite Kennedy's much vaunted declaration that the Alliance was "an alliance of free governments" .' The United States soon reverted to reliance on rightwing military regimes which used repression of the most extreme variety. Moreover, the conditions the United States AID attached to its aid practise followed closely those demanded by the IMF; at the end of a list of public expenditure cuts, wage cuts, trade and exchange liberalisation measures, devaluation and so on, there might be a reference, couched in rather vague terms, to the desirability of land reform.

It is clear that the policies to be promoted by aid are not to involve any direct and radical attack on the causes of poverty. Even without such an attack, it is difficult to see how any government, which attempted with any vigour to redistribute income within the country, could acquiesce in massive international inequality or sit idly by while the country's resources and capital were drained away by foreigners. Such a government would be an unreliable ally for the 'aid' agencies and would probably end up being opposed by them; there are plenty of examples of reformist or populist governments being subjected to destabilisation and eventual destruction. It is exceedingly unlikely that any government in an underdeveloped country will act to eradicate poverty except under the pressure, and with the assistance, of a major popular mobilisation. This would be much too dangerous for the interests of the industrialised countries for it to be tolerated, let alone encouraged.

The fact is that reforms are a luxury that can be afforded in rich and prosperous countries — in effect in those countries whose ruling classes have been able to enrich themselves at the expense of the rest of the world. Few countries in the Third World, with the exception of those that possess oil in large quantities, are in that position. In other countries there are, indeed, some extremely wealthy elites. But their position and their wealth is precarious and maintained only on the basis of brutal exploitation of their own peoples. It is clear that, in the last analysis, the weight of the aid agencies, such as it is, will be on the side of these people rather than on the side of the impoverished masses who threaten their existence and that of their foreign allies.

Industrialisation

Industrialisation, in one form or another, is undoubtedly one of the prerequisites for escape from underdevelopment. But industrialisation in the dependent areas has been, at least until recently, systematically discouraged by the industrialised countries and their agencies. The governments of underdeveloped countries have been given all kinds of good advice, based on apparently unimpeachable doctrines of 'comparative advantage', to the effect that they should concentrate on what they are supposed to be good at: the production of raw materials and primary commodities.

Foreign investments by multinational companies did not finance industrialisation. The metropolitan powers had destroyed industries in the territories they dominated; they continued to ensure that industrialisation, which might compete with their industries and deprive them of markets, did not take place. Import duties in developed countries were, and are, commonly higher on processed than on unprocessed goods. Restrictive quotas are applied on such products as cheap textiles, which threaten to disrupt metropolitan industry. At the same time, the developed countries continue to insist, through institutions such as the World Bank and the IMF, on the advantages of free trade — for others. The governments of underdeveloped countries are told, in no uncertain terms, and with a wealth of supporting neo-classical theory, how much it would be to their own advantage to abolish protection and give free entry to the products of the industrialised countries.

Industrialisation in the dominated areas has, until recently, mainly taken the form of so-called import-substitution: the manufacture locally of goods that were previously imported. The growth of import-substituting industries, particularly in some Latin American countries, received an impetus especially during the two world wars and during the Great Depression of the 1930s, when metropolitan manufactured goods became unavailable. It has also taken place as a result of high protective tariffs against certain manufactured goods in some underdeveloped countries, especially since the second world war. These have forced metropolitan manufacturers themselves to build, for example, car assembly plants in several Latin American and other countries in order to preserve their markets, because the import duties on bits of cars are commonly much lower than they are on whole cars. The problem with such import-substituting industry is that it is often very inefficient because it relies on highly protected markets, and underdeveloped countries end up not only buying very expensive cars, but sometimes having to pay more in foreign exchange than they would have to do if they imported the cars, soft drinks, or whatever, directly. Moreover, since it is politically more difficult to close down a factory than it is to restrict 'inessential' imports, the country is left with a bill, possibly higher, for 'essential' imports of raw materials and parts to make the 'inessential' goods whose import was previously restricted. This does nothing to alter the distribution of production and resources, which continue to cater primarily for the previous consumption patterns of a small elite. When the investment was made by a foreign company, there was normally no prospect of increasing the markets for the goods produced by exporting some of them, since the foreign company was not interested in setting up competition against itself. Vaitsos, in his study of Andean Pact countries, says that over 80 per cent of the contracts he was able to study contained clause specifically prohibiting exports to other countries.

But in the last 10 to 20 years there has been a change: there have been quite big increases in exports of manufactured goods from some underdeveloped countries. They are apparently no longer naturally destined merely to hew wood and draw water; they can make television sets as well. There is now, in the orthodox literature, a new category of countries: the NICs, or Newly Industrialising Countries. Over a third of the exports of 'middle income' countries now consists of manufactured goods, whereas in 1960 they were only about 14 per cent of exports. About 19 per cent of the exports of 'low income' countries are now manufactured goods. In some countries, the growth of such exports has been startling: the annual growth rate of industrial exports between 1960 and 1971 was 30 per cent for Brazil, 18 per cent for Hong Kong, 21 per cent for Mexico, 60 per cent for South Korea, and 35 per cent for Taiwan. It is said that there is now a new international division of labour, in which labour-intensive manufacturing is increasingly carried out in underdeveloped countries, where wages are low.

Multinational companies have become interested in locating the more labour-intensive parts of their manufacturing processes in underdeveloped countries in order to take advantage of the extreme cheapness of labour there. Previously, one of the solutions to the problem, for capitalists, of high wages and strong trade-union organisation in the developed countries had been to import cheaper labour into Europe from the Mediterranean, the Caribbean and Asia, and into the United States from Mexico. But such immigrant workers have to be housed, have to be given access to social services, and are the object of racial attacks and abuse. It appears now to be considered easier — and with improved transport and communications, practicable — for the labour of the peoples of underdeveloped countries to be used overseas. Attempts are therefore being made to get rid of the immigrants, not just because of the depression and high levels of unemployment in metropolitan countries, but also because some of the work they were doing has been transferred overseas. The problem of course affects local workers as well, but immigrant workers are usually the first to suffer. Some of the textile products which were previously made mainly by Asians in sweat shops in Bradford are now being imported directly from India, Hong Kong, Singapore and other Asian countries, as well as Southern European countries such as Spain and Portugal.

The idea is that the machines should be taken to the workers rather than the other way round. Radios, televisions and cameras, as well as textiles, are being imported on an increasing scale from 'low wage' countries. In the electronics industry, it now pays multinational companies to have the assembly of some parts, for example silicon chips, carried out in underdeveloped countries, while other parts of the process continue to be carried out in the metropolitan countries. This new need to locate manufacturing in countries where labour is cheap is particularly acute for firms based in the United States, where wages are so much higher than elsewhere that they found themselves unable to compete with the Japanese and even the Germans. Underdeveloped countries thus become 'export platforms', in the phrase of Celso Furtado, for products which are consumed in the United States and Europe much as the products of the mines and plantations are. These products lower the cost of manufacturing in the metropolitan countries by providing cheap components or cheap 'wage goods', thus making it easier to keep wages down.

Firms are also making the discovery that in underdeveloped countries, contrary to previous assertions in orthodox literature, not only are wages low, but, as the United States Tariff commission reported in 1973, levels of productivity are approximately the same in similar types of industry. There are additional 'advantages': less strict controls on pollution levels, fewer safety regulations, longer hours worked, better 'labour discipline' or, in other words, more repression and, above all, less protection for the workers from trade unions. This is presumably what the Brandt Report has in mind when it says that developing countries

> constitute in a sense a new economic frontier, with fewer of the special economic difficulties and social and political constraints operating in the North.

This moving out of manufacturing from developed to underdeveloped areas where labour is cheaper has caused some concern about loss of jobs in developed countries, particularly of course among workers and their unions. Workers in British factories have seen their products displaced by cheap exports from Asia and have demanded import controls. The highly conservative North American trade unions have not only demanded import control but have also begun to see that it is in their interest to show some solidarity with oppressed workers outside the United States. Having actively collaborated with the CIA to assist subservient 'free' trade unions in underdeveloped countries and even to promote the process of de-stabilisation in Chile, they now talk of a boycott of trade with the Pinochet regime because they see jobs in the United States threatened by the extremely low wages made possible by the repression in Chile. Similarly, as Richard J. Barnet and Ronald E. Muller point out in their book *Global Reach:*

> United States union leaders begin to realise that the army, 34,000 strong, of 30-cents-an-hour child labourers in Hong Kong is not only a sin to be deplored at the annual convention but a real and growing economic threat to American workers.

And they add:

> Corporate organisation on a world scale is a highly effective weapon for undercutting the power of organised labour everywhere. Capital, technology, and marketplace ideology, the bases of corporate power, are mobile; workers, by and large, are not.

As evidence that this new corporate weapon is used, they say:

> Perhaps the most celebrated example is the strike at Ford's British operation in 1970. After a summit conference with the Prime Minister, Henry Ford II delivered a stiff note to the British people. 'We have got hundreds of millions of pounds invested in Great Britain and we can't recommend any new capital investment in a country constantly dogged with labour problems. There is nothing wrong with Ford of Britain but with the country'. Shortly thereafter he shifted back to Ohio a proposed £30-million operation for building Pinto engines. The following year he pointedly announced that Ford's major new plant would be put in Spain, a country that offered 'social peace'.

There is thus a new twist to the theory of comparative advantage: underdeveloped countries are said to have the 'advantage' of very low wages. In fact they are advised, by experts from the World Bank, the International Monetary Fund and elsewhere, to make use of this 'advantage' in order to attract foreign investment and to promote exports of manufactured goods. The theory is that underdeveloped countries should remove restrictions on imports, devalue their currencies and keep down wages, and that they will then be able to produce very cheap and competitive exports. This is seen in part as a response to the chronic balance-of-payments problems of underdeveloped countries into which their dependence on the imperial powers has led them; if they cannot earn foreign exchange through exports, then they will not be able to pay for imports, finance the outflow of profits, or repay their foreign debts. The fact that precisely the countries with the greatest 'success' in increasing exports of manufactured goods (for example Brazil, Mexico and South Korea) have the most massive debt problems has not so far dented their new-found enthusiasm for manufactured exports. Thus the World Bank's confidential Report on Indonesia, quoted in the *Far Eastern Economic Review*, noted:

> To get the industrial sector going on a sound basis with as little protection as possible and with considerable export orientation is now perhaps the single most important overall policy requirement.

And, the report adds, 'this will require an increase in the level of private industrial foreign capital flows.'

Such a policy clearly accords with the interests of multinational companies. It does conflict with some other metropolitan interests, for example the textile industry. But as this new 'international division of labour' develops, older industries such as the textile industry in advanced capitalist countries have shown some ability to adapt and modernise into more specialised and advanced forms of production. Their governments are urged, by the Brandt Report for instance, to assist in this process:

> Protectionism certainly leads in the wrong direction for it helps to maintain — at considerable cost — structures that are becoming obsolete. It stops people from adapting to new forms of the international division of labour and postpones essential decisions.

Japan is held out as an example. It has probably been more successful than most industrialised countries in implementing this logic and moving rapidly into the new technologies. A report from the Japanese Ministry of Trade explains it thus: Japan should retain 'high technology and knowledge-intensive industries', which yield 'high added value', while industries 'such as textiles which involve a low degree of processing and generate low added value [would] be moved to developing countries where costs are low'. The textile industry has been described as 'structurally depressed' and the Japanese Industrial Structure Council has advised the industry to get out of traditional fields and to concentrate on high quality fabrics and fashion goods. Less dynamic industrial countries like Britain find it more difficult to adjust and to retain their leadership in the technological race; the end result of the policies of the Thatcher government could well be deindustrialisation, rather than any new dynamic industry rising from the ruins of the old.

These developments have led some to argue that the prospects for industrialisation in underdeveloped countries are better than they were 20 years ago. At that time, it was widely believed, by the left in particular, that industrialisation under capitalism in these dependent countries would be impossible: their own capitalists were too weak and dependent and were in any case mainly interested in making money from the import-export business, speculation in real estate, crumbs from the multinationals and Swiss bank accounts; foreign investors were not interested in creating competition for themselves. Now, not only are multinationals investing in manufacturing in underdeveloped countries on a considerable scale, but there is much evidence that the elites of underdeveloped countries are themselves investing their money in manufacturing enterprises. Many of the factories producing textiles, footwear and so on are locally owned. The *Review of African Political Economy* devoted its issue No. 8 to 'Capitalism in Africa'; some of its authors argued that there exists in many countries in Africa an entrepreneurial class investing in manufacturing industry independently of the multinational companies. Some underdeveloped countries, including India and Brazil, have their 'own' multinational companies. Bill Warren, in an article in *New Left Review* and in his book *Imperialism: Pioneer of Capitalism* dismissed most the the arguments of the 'dependency' school of thought and argued that independent industrialisation under capitalism in underdeveloped countries was possible (while pointing out that this was not the same thing as 'ideal' development with full employment, diversified agriculture and industry, good housing, equality, and so on).

But much of the New Industrialisation is of a particular

type. It certainly cannot be equated with balanced, independent industrialisation, catering for the needs of the peoples of underdeveloped countries. It remains true that much of it is the result of investment by multinational companies and that the new industries are to a great extent export industries. As such they have disadvantages in addition to an outflow of profits. Very often the new manufacturing activities take place in so-called Export Processing Zones, where production is almost exclusively for export. These zones are usually cut off from the rest of the country, physically by concrete walls and barbed wire, and economically and legally by the special conditions given to multinational companies investing in them: tax holidays, freedom from tariffs and duties, freedom to repatriate profits, freedom from protective labour legislation, special immunity from strikes and other forms of protest, an abundant supply of cheap and 'docile' labour. The governments of underdeveloped countries, desperate for foreign exchange, compete among themselves for the favours of foreign investors; often the inducements are so high that the foreign exchange gains themselves become rather illusory. The Export Processing Zones, furthermore, absorb resources which might otherwise be used for the development of agriculture and industry for the benefit of local people rather than for that of foreigners. Thus many of the new industries cater to the needs of the metropolis in ways very similar to the mines and plantations and are in much the same sense an 'outpost of the mother country'.

The exporting firms tend to have few relations with the rest of the economy apart from employing some workers; they are integrated, instead, into the structures of multinational companies. Even if they are not actually subsidiaries of a multinational company, what they produce may be saleable only to the multinational company that commissioned the product, and they may also be exclusively dependent on inputs from the same source; this means that their bargaining power is minimal and that they have no control over what they produce, where they sell it, how much they sell it for, what they produce it with, or what they pay for what they produce it with.

These export processing activities are thus highly vulnerable to the actions of multinational firms. The latter are notoriously 'footloose'. If the supply of labour shows signs of becoming less docile or more expensive, they can move elsewhere. As a Malaysian trade unionist reported:

> The firms have also let us know that in case of labour trouble or wage demands, they can stop production within a month and transfer to another neighbouring country with a cheaper labour force in the Asian area.

Sometimes they move when their tax holidays runs out. Japan has apparently developed a barge on which factories can be floated to new sources of cheap labour once a particular lot has been used up. In some cases the workers are 'used up' in a rather literal sense. The assembly of silicon chips requires detailed work under a microscope; after three years the eyesight of the workers, mainly women, begins to fail; 'granma, where are your glasses?' is a common greeting to electronics workers over 25 years old in Hong Kong.

Because most of the products are exported to the industrialised countries, they are also very dependent on economic conditions there. There is the possibility that, as the depression reduces consumption in these countries and as more of the underdeveloped countries attempt to enter the business of exporting manufactures, their markets will dry up. In addition, the metropolitan governments may be deaf to the pleas against protection. There are already plenty of examples of quotas being used to restrict cheap imports; these restrictions may become more severe as the threat to domestic industries becomes greater. A sign of the times may be that, at a recent seminar attended by the high priests of free trade, these North American economists were beginning to change their tune; 'orderly marketing' and 'organised free trade' might after all be accomodated in their theory. The theory of comparative advantage is not so useful when the comparative advantage turns out to be with your competitors!

Another problem is that, as progress towards automation proceeds, some manufacturing processes may become less labour-intensive and they may again be transferred back to the developed countries. Workers everywhere are vulnerable to changes in technology, but they are probably particularly so in underdeveloped countries. Whatever the willingness of multinational companies to move manufacturing jobs around the world, they retain most of their highly skilled and most lucrative activities in the countries in which they are based. About 96 per cent of 'research and development' activity is said by the Brandt Report to be carried out in developed countries. Nearly all of the top managers of the multinational companies are nationals of the country in which they are based. They maintain a rigidly centralised and hierarchical organisation in which the major decisions are all taken in the 'home' country, and as little as possible of the technology and marketing expertise, and almost none of the research, is transferred to underdeveloped countries. So long as they continue to control around a third of world trade, the international division of labour is likely to imply a kind of hierarchy analogous to that within societies: the more skilled and lucrative activities will be located in the industrial centres, and the labouring will be done, for very low rewards, in the periphery.

Worst of all, the very existence of manufacturing for export in underdeveloped countries appears, for the moment at any rate, to be dependent on what can only be called the super-exploitation of labour. Unlike the previous forms of import-substituting manufacturing, it is not in any way dependent on the creation or maintenance of an internal market, and therefore provides no reason for the redistribution of income, even to the middle classes. On the contrary, its existence depends on government policies to secure an ample supply of cheap labour. As the *Investor's Guide*, published by the Zona Franca Industrial y Comercial de Cartagena in Colombia, explicitly states:

> Low Cost Labour: this is without doubt the chief incentive offered by the ZFIC as the salaries are more or less the same as those that prevail in the industrial zones of the Far East ... Male and female workers are easily obtained due to high rate of unemployment, rapid increase of population and the emigration from rural zones to the cities.

The austerity measures promoted as a means of adjusting to crushing debts and balance-of-payments problems have as a by-product, intentional or otherwise, the addition of many more destitute people to the reserve army of unemployed for foreign investors to use. Real wages decline even further, and governments cut such social expenditures as there were which, very partially, alleviated the suffering caused by low wages and unemployment.

Wages and conditions are sometimes, but not always, better in multinational firms than they are in small local firms; workers earning wages in foreign companies are sometimes — very misleadingly — referred to as an 'aristocracy of labour'. Like the plantation workers in colonial times and since, the workers in the new export industries often receive wages that barely provide for their own subsistence. They are not paid enough to support their families, and even, in some cases, may themselves have to be supported by the work of their families on the land or in the so-called 'informal sector' of small workshops and petty trading. Thus the export processing industries receive effectively subsidised labour. In addition, multinational companies take people at their fittest and cheapest and discard them when they become disabled, ill, old or merely exhausted through too great pressure of work. They hire apprentices and fire them when their 'apprenticeship' ends; they sack workers just before they are entitled to any security of employment or minimum wages; increasingly, they hire children and sack them before they are entitled to adult wages; some 80 to 90 per cent of workers in Export Processing Zones are women, who are cheaper than men; the women, and men, are hired when they are young and fired when they are worn out, say at 30 years; the preponderant age range of those employed is 14 to 24 years old; and a 50 to 100 per cent turnover of labour a year is common. In Hong Kong, a British colony where British labour legislation nevertheless does not apply, 34,000 children work, half of them a 10-hour day.

Hours of work are in general very long. In Hong Kong again, 60 per cent of adults work a seven-day week. In South Korea, which is a 'model' of export promotion, a 1976 *International Herald Tribune* headline read: 'Seven-day, 84 Hour Work Weeks: Seoul's economic miracle is a heavy burden on workers'. According to a special edition of *AMPO*:

The workers take 'pep-pills' (known as 'Timing') ... Most

bus-conductors in Seoul work 18 hours a day ... We work from five in the morning to one or two o'clock at night ... I fall asleep in the galloping bus ... At the garment factories ... workers ... usually work for 14 to 16 hours a day. In peak demand periods, they are frequently asked to work two or three days without any sleep.

In the metallurgical industry in Sao Paolo workers work 11 to 12 hours a day; some work 12 hours a day, seven days a week. Workers also spend long hours travelling to work on desperately overcrowded buses; the *average* time spent this way in Sao Paolo, according to a trade unionist reported in the *International Herald Tribune*, is six hours a day. In Chile they can no longer afford bus fares; they have to walk. And holidays are minimal.

Since the productivity of labour in underdeveloped countries, or the amount produced in a particular time, is increasingly recognised to be similar to that in the developed countries, and since the machinery used is quite often less or inferior or second-hand, it is likely that people in underdeveloped countries, far from being 'lazy' or inefficient, as is sometimes supposed, often work harder and more efficiently than their fellow-workers in developed countries. This is partly, of course, because firms can make harsher demands on them with greater impunity. One example is that women in underdeveloped countries sometimes do electronic assembly work with the naked eye for which workers in the United States have to be supplied with microscopes. Thus multinational companies investing in underdeveloped countries benefit not only from longer hours worked, but also from greater intensity of work during those hours.

This, together with generally poor conditions at work, manifests itself in a greater incidence of accidents at work and resulting disabilities. ILO statistics show the highest accident rates are in underdeveloped export-promoting countries, followed, in that order, by other underdeveloped countries, the capitalist industrialised countries, and the 'centrally planned economies'. The accident rates given for South Korea are, more or less consistently, the highest in the world and in some cases five and 10 times higher than in other underdeveloped countries. The reasons given by workers for the high rate of accidents, in South Korea and elsewhere, are excessive fatigue, not enough food, speed up of the assembly line. In the Massam Free Export Zone of South Korea accidents occur at the rate of 4,500 a year for 24,000 employees, or at a rate of 19 per cent in a workforce 75 per cent of whom are women. 'Such a high rate of industrial accidents,' says *AMPO* 'is a direct result of the pressure for high intensity work exerted by companies which enter Korea to exploit cheap labour-intensive production.' This and similar occurrences no doubt have something to do with the fact that, in this 'model' of rapid development in a militantly anti-communist country, there was a major rebellion in 1980 which had to be put down with government troops.

Finally, wages. Information on wage rates is scattered and unreliable. But the following are some examples. In similar activities in the electronics industry, hourly rates of pay are reported to be US$0.27 in Hong Kong and US$3.13 in the United States; in semi-conductors they are reported as US$0.33 in Korea, US$0.29 in Singapore, US$0.30 in Jamaica, and around three dollars an hour in the United States. In other underdeveloped countries, wage rates are lower. Textile workers in the Philippines are reported to gross US$672 a year. In Calcutta, printers are said to make between US$18 and US$28 a *month*, and other workers US$10 a month or less, for a 10- to 12-hour day. Daily wages for unskilled labour were certified by an accounting firm as US$1.90 in South Korea, US$1.45 in Indonesia, and US$1.75 in the Philippines. Minimum wage rates, where they exist, are little enforced and are in any case often declining in real terms. It seems fairly clear that wages are also doing so. The World Bank is said to be opposed to minimum wage legislation. One result of these low wages is that, for some large firms, the wage bill amounts to only seven per cent of sales receipts, while profits amount to between a quarter and a third.

It is thus doubtful, to say the least, whether the recent growth in manufactured exports can be said to be of benefit to the peoples of underdeveloped countries. They are, much as before, doing the dirty work of the West, and they are being unmercifully exploited. The increase in export-processing activities in underdeveloped countries is a special phenomenon; it is not a balanced process of industrial growth. As before, the economies of the underdeveloped countries are appendages of those of the metropolitan powers and function in their interest. There are some who ask themselves how it is that, say, an apparently decent Canadian manager of a multinational company can treat his workers with such ruthless disregard. The answer is that he does it because he is able to do it: the reserve army of workers is there and waiting, because for the time being they have no other way of surviving. In addition, in most underdeveloped countries, the supposedly blind forces of the market are, in reality, much helped by the repressive apparatus of the state, which in turn is aided by the West.

Repression and Foreign Support For It

Intervention by the state authorities is widely used to ensure the continued supply of cheap labour and to crush attempts to organise for better wages and conditions. This intervention is openly and enthusiastically welcomed in the West, whatever their protestations about freedom and democracy. The following examples, most of them taken from newspaper quotations assembled by André Gunder Frank for a chapter in his forthcoming book *Crisis: In the Third World* give some idea of the extent of the repression of working class organisation and the connivance of the West.

The World Bank report on Indonesia already quoted from the *Far Eastern Economic Review* enthusiastically recommends Indonesia as a place for multinationals to invest in:

> Indonesia has the largest remaining pool of inexpensive and relatively literate labour in East Asia. Even before the recent devaluation, wages for unskilled labour were among the lowest in the world; lower than in Singapore, Hong Kong, South Korea and Taiwan. Labour is not unionised.

In fact, Indonesia has one of the most notoriously repressive regimes, responsible for the murder of many thousands of

Communist supporters and the continuing imprisonment and torture of many thousands more. It is one of the major recipients of Western aid. In South Korea, the penalty for striking is a prison sentence of up to seven years:

> low wages are crucial to export goals and government officials admit it ... this means labour law and order: no strikes, no minimum wage, no unemployment compensation, no meaningful industrial safety regulations ... Even the World Bank referred to 'the extraordinary influence that government agencies can exert on wage settlements' [downward, presumably]. South Korea's few significant labour unions are reliably reported to have been infiltrated by the Korean Central Intelligence Agency. (*International Herald Tribune*, 30 May 1977)

President Marcos of the Philippines decreed as follows:

> It is the policy of the State to encourage trade unionism and free collective bargaining within the framework of compulsory and voluntary arbitration and therefore all forms of strike, picketing and lockouts are hereby strictly prohibited.

In the Philippines, real wages between 1965 and 1976 for skilled and unskilled workers declined by 35 and 29 per cent respectively, according to Central Bank statistics. Hong Kong's industry is 'virtually free of strikes'. In Singapore:

> Investors can expect that the lid will be kept on wages for some time. The Singapore Government and the organised labour movement under its firm control are making a special effort to restore the island's attractiveness as a low-wage centre. (*Far Eastern Economic Review*, 14 May 1976)

In Thailand: 'one of the major objectives of the military junta ... is ... to re-establish investor confidence. Although the trade-union movement has not formally been declared illegal, strikes are now forbidden and a purge of unions has begun.' (IPC, 25 November 1976). 'Oh, it's just wonderful. We used to have terrible problems with the unions. Now when they give us any trouble the Government just puts them in jail.' (a member of the Oberoi family in India, quoted in *The New York Times* magazine, 4 April 1976). In Pakistan, on 10 July 1977, Chief Martial Law Administrator General Zia ul Haq issued Martial Law Regulation No. 12 which stated: 'all kinds of activity relating or pertaining to, or connected in any manner whatsoever with trade unions, labour associations or any other body of similar nature is prohibited.' 'I have great respect for the institution of elections,' said Zia in 1977, reported in the *International Herald Tribune*, 'but I cannot allow the country to face disaster for their sake.' By 'disaster' Zia meant a landslide victory for the deposed party of Bhutto, who had taken some measures hostile to foreign investment, and whom Zia had had executed.

> Some observers in Bangladesh are talking of the possibility of an Indonesian-style 'crackdown solution' to the dilemma. The most recent executions are seen as only a prelude to what might develop. The arrival of the British Military Advisory Team [is] seen ... as not unrelated to securing a confident 'stable' environment agreeable to foreign investing interests. The British are deeply involved along with the Americans in the proposed investment schemes ... Mass executions of the imprisoned ordered by the central authority of the State is something repugnantly new. (*Economic and Political Weekly*, 25 March 1978)

> Egypt has a surplus of employable labour. In these inflationary times, Egypt retains its significant wage-cost advantage over many other developing countries. (An Egyptian government announcement in *African Development* 1977)

> Egyptians voted today to approve or reject a decree of repressive law-and-order measures signed by President Anwar Sadat in the aftermath of the bloody and destructive bread riots last month ...
>
> The measures include hard labour for life for strikes, sit-ins, demonstrations, obstruction to government activities and 'causing damage to public or private property'. (*New York Times*, 10 February 1977)

The extent of the repression in Chile after the military coup against Allende, the savage cuts in wages, employment and living standards and the opening of Chile to foreign investment, with the so far unfulfilled expectation that this will lead to growth in the export of manufactured goods, is well known. The Director of Quimica Hoechst de Chile, in a letter to his Home Office in Frankfurt in September 1973, commented: 'the long awaited intervention of the military finally occurred ... We believe that the action of the military and the police could not have been planned and co-ordinated more intelligently.' In Argentina, after the military coup against Isabel Peron, the outlook for foreign investment brightened.

> The military is cracking down on labour leaders in a move to break their stranglehold on the formation of economic policy. Unions have been suspended and most key Peronist labour leaders jailed ... The brunt of the anti-inflation drive will probably be born by wage earners. (BLA, 24 March 1976)

> International organisations like the IMF, the World Bank, and the Inter-American Development Bank, as well as commercial banks in the United States, Western Europe and Japan, have carefully studied and evaluated the combination of economic policies of the new [Argentinian] government. Organisations in both categories have praised the policies and their results in the most practical of ways, by granting loan guarantees to support the national plans. (US Department of Commerce)

In Bolivia wages never recovered from the 1972 devaluation, when most wage earners lost about 40 per cent of their purchasing power.

> [US Ambassador] Boeker and the government are in full agreement ... on the threat posed by the reorganisation of the labour movement, and the demand for general and considerable wage rises ... David Blanco, the economy minister ... reported that IMF officials had told him that a general increase in wages of the levels being suggested would be 'suicidal'. (LAPR 17 March 1978)

The repression is, of course, not only directed against trade unions or attempts to organise them. It is used against opposition, or 'subversive forces', of all types, which in general run far greater risks of imprisonment, torture and death than they do in prosperous Western countries. This is because of the inability, or unwillingness, of most governments in the Third World to deal with the problems of extreme poverty and inequality in any other way. With the sometimes covert support of the West, and to the extent that they are able to do so, the governments of the developing so-called 'free world' crush opposition and prohibit attempts to organise it.

Many of them are following in the wake of colonial regimes, which used similarly repressive measures to deal with opposition and to maintain the supply of cheap labour. Direct colonial rule has become impossible to sustain, except in a few small areas. The colonial peoples have been driven, by injustice, neglect and material deprivation, to rebel against it. Sometimes independence was won only after considerable periods of armed struggle; sometimes the metropolitan powers, seeing the writing on the wall, handed over power more or less peacefully. But all is not yet lost for the West. In most parts of the world, colonial regimes have been replaced by similarly autocratic neo-colonial regimes, whose economic policies are not strikingly different from those of their predecessors and whose members have an interest in the continuation of the system and, in fact, in simply taking over some of the privileges enjoyed by their predecessors.

Often these regimes have lost much of the popular support they originally had, and are kept in power by military means, even if the government is not actually run by the army. But generally the force is not now wielded directly from abroad by gunships and marines, but by local armies and police forces, most of which are however armed, trained and equipped by former colonial powers or by the United States. The United States alone has trained almost 400,000 military men and over a million policemen. A conscious effort is made to ensure that the people trained in the West, both in the military and repressive arts and in other fields, become friends and allies against Communist subversion. The United States and its allies have many friends among the ruling elites. Alliances shift. Traditionally, there has been an alliance between land-owners, who are interested in agricultural exports and in cheap imports of luxury goods, and foreign private investors; local manufacturers have sometimes been hostile to foreigners, who threaten them with take-overs and bankruptcy, but they are also often prepared to throw in their lot with the multinationals, who offer them comfortable salaries and a certain show of prestige; government officials can be bribed and won over, directly by foreign companies and less directly by official aid agencies on the look-out for 'our men'; and governments themselves usually know very well which side their bread is buttered, for it is certain that the West can come to their support in subversive times with offers of military and financial aid, temporary rescue from their debt problems, and an assurance that at least some imports will continue to flow.

Perhaps the most eloquent scourge of these neo-colonial elites was the West Indian, Franz Fanon, who took part in the Algerian liberation struggle: he describes them derisively as 'sort of little greedy caste, avid and voracious, with the mind of a huckster, only too glad to accept the dividends that the former colonial power hands out to it'. Such people will make resounding statements at international conferences, will demand a New International Economic Order, will agree verbally that the imperialists are mercilessly exploiting their people. But, if faced with radical choices, they would rather, as one of them put it, be 'ground under the heel of imperialism', for the simple reason that they would rather retain the privileges of office and the delights of luxury consumption.

When, however, these people do rebel against their subservience to the West, or are themselves defeated by popular forces, the West is quick to intervene. A recurrent phenomenon is for anti-imperialist or left-leaning regimes to be overthrown by military coups, which then establish right-wing repressive regimes; the West is frequently involved in the engineering of these coups and in any case welcomes the new regimes with aid and other assistance. Thus Sukarno, Nasser, Goulart, N'Krumah, Allende and many others were overthrown in this way. The techniques used by the West, now sometimes known as 'de-stabilisation', include the denial of aid, private credit and imports, and the financing and arming of internal opposition. Such techniques were, for example, recently used in Jamaica and they contributed to the defeat of the Manley government in the 1980 elections. An article by Edward Heath in the London *Times*, welcoming the election results, can be considered representative of relatively enlightened sections of the Western ruling classes: Heath maintains, rather remarkably, that the Jamaican people voted for 'an economic philosophy more attentive to the needs of foreign — particularly Western — investors and less governed by State direction of the means of production'. Jamaica, Heath continues, must be protected against 'aggression by foreign powers' [Cuba or Russia?] and 'Cuban-inspired subversion':

> It would of course be politically unacceptable in today's world for the United States or for any other western country directly to intervene against ... externally provoked subversion — although it is sobering to recall that President Johnson did so in the Dominican Republic in 1965 without provoking any challenge. There is therefore no alternative to effective indigenous security arrangements if stability is to be maintained in the Caribbean ...
>
> The West must encourage this by providing ... the necessary equipment for reconnaissance, policing and paramilitary intervention.
>
> But we cannot leave our security policy in the Caribbean at that. There is no substitute for the West's own military power as a source of psychological reassurance for our friends and in deterring threats against which their own defence capabilities would not be adequate.

'The West's own military power' has been used against governments or popular forces considered hostile to the interests of the West on many occasions since the second world war: in Algeria, Egypt, Jordan, Lebanon, Iran, Malaysia, Gabon, the Congo, Uganda, Tanzania, Chad, the Dominican Republic, Guatemala, Anguilla, Trinidad, Ireland, etc. In addition, nearly all of the countries in which revolutions have taken place have been subjected to military intervention from the West. The precedent was set for this when troops from fourteen different countries were involved in attempts to put down the Russian revolution between 1918 and 1921. The United States has fought wars in Korea and Indochina and organised the abortive Bay of Pigs landing in Cuba.

Military intervention is, however, a last resort. Economic weapons are generally used first — and, of course, afterwards. Aid and normal sources of credit from the West dry up. Vietnam, whose economy and agriculture were devastated by the American war, has made many fruitless appeals for official and private loans from the West to help in reconstruction. At the Paris Agreements of 1973, the United States undertook to pay a war indemnity of more than £3,000 million over five years; none of it has been paid, and the Carter administration secured the withdrawal of World bank and other foreign assistance. The loans that have been made are token compared to the money that poured into Saigon when the Americans were there.

The sequence of events in Cuba was as follows. The Cubans were offered cheaper oil by the Soviet union. The United States-owned refineries refused to process it. The Cuban government nationalised the refineries. The United States government responded with a total trade embargo which had not been lifted by early 1981, including a ban on sugar imports from Cuba which the United States had previously bought at a preferential price. Practically all of Cuba's existing machinery and equipment was North American and spare parts became totally unavailable. The Cubans were reduced to feats of improvisation and to the adaptation of goods supplied by the Soviet Union and Eastern Europe.

Other post-revolutionary or leftist governments elsewhere have suffered from the non-availability of commercial credit and spare parts, in addition to having official aid cut. 'I don't see why we should stand by and watch a country go Communist due to the irresponsibility of its own people.' Thus Kissinger, defender of freedom and democracy, on Chile. The United States did its best, mainly by funding Christian Democracy, to make sure that Allende was not elected in Chile. When he was nevertheless elected, ITT produced a plot to stop him taking office. Popular Unity nevertheless took office and governed according to the constitution. There was more freedom of expression, less imprisonment of political opponents under

Allende than anywhere in Latin America at the time or under previous governments in Chile. As Allende said at the United Nations in 1972, Chile was then 'a country of unlimited cultural, religious and ideological tolerance and where there is no room for racial discrimination'. The Popular Unity government was cautious in its treatment of private interests and decided to take on all of its predecessors' commercial debts; its foreign creditors would not agree to any renegotiation of the debts and Chile therefore paid them off more promptly than a right-wing government would have had to. Commercial credits were reduced from $220 million to $30 million and aid from the United States AID, the World Bank and other international organisations, which had amounted to about $130 million a year, was reduced to nil; World Bank loans for projects which had already been agreed with the previous administration were stopped. This was done before the announcement that the government had decided to subtract the copper companies' estimated super-profits from any sums it might have paid them in compensation; and the decision to nationalise the copper companies was taken by a unanimous decision of the Chilean political parties represented in Congress.

People in the West muttered darkly that elections would never be held again and hoped presumably that, if elections were held, these and other CIA/ITT 'de-stabilisation' measures would cause Popular Unity to lose them. Municipal elections were held, and the Popular Unity increased its vote. The Chilean armed forces and their friends in the West then decided that elections must not after all be held. When the democratically-elected Popular Unity government was overthrown by a brutal military coup, money from the West, in particular from the World Bank and the US/AID, began to flow again and the Chilean debt was renegotiated on favourable terms under the auspices of the IMF. The Pinochet regime that took over has been so bad that the Ford administration was forced by the United States Congress and civil rights pressures to reduce official aid and stop military aid. But private, mainly United States, banks came to the rescue and increased their loans to Chile by over 500 per cent in 1976. Chile had, after all, rejoined the Western camp.

Resistance

In spite of these pressures, resistance is widespread. The peoples of underdeveloped countries have not passively accepted injustice and oppression. The extent of the repression indeed supposes that there is also much to repress and that the opposition is strong.

Resistance began during the colonial period. The peoples of Indochina, China, Algeria, the former Portuguese colonies of Africa won their independence from colonial or semi-colonial rule after long armed struggles, with guerilla forces fighting against the armies of their rulers. In Kenya, Malaysia and Zimbabwe there was armed resistance against the British or British settlers. Colonial history was indeed punctuated by rebellions, perhaps the best known of which is the Indian Mutiny of 1857 when many thousands of the British governing classes were killed and which was put down by the British in an orgy of retaliatory atrocities. The British fought many battles in India; the granting of political independence to India was forced on a reluctant Labour government after the second world war. Latin Americans won their independence from Spain in protracted battles in the early nineteenth century. Political leaders demanding independence were imprisoned with great frequency: Kenyatta, N'Krumah, Gandhi and many others spent periods in British gaols. In some countries, for example in Nigeria, there were major working class strikes and struggles for better conditions before the second world war; and there were many more strikes, rebellions and forms of rural resistance throughout Africa after the war.

More recently, there has been armed resistance to many contemporary right-wing governments. In practically every Latin American country there have been guerilla activities of one form or another, often for prolonged periods. In Argentina the urban guerilla forces, who had considerable links with the organised working class, at times seemed near to defeating the military regime. There is armed struggle in many parts of Africa: in Namibia, in Eritrea, in Chad, and already in South Africa. Guerilla forces have been active in India, in Thailand, in the Philippines, in Timor. There have also been, in many countries, demonstrations accompanied by violent repression, strikes whose leaders have been executed and imprisoned, clandestine resistance of many varieties including the illegal distribution of newspapers and leaflets, organisation to resist the destruction of working class neighbourhoods, the formation of trade unions and other banned or illegal organisations, kidnapping, hijacking, and so on.

In many cases the leadership and support for these activities has been of marxist inspiration. In other cases the resistance that is the object of repression is asking for liberal reforms or merely a change of government: Bhutto was executed in Pakistan and Kim Dae Jung was sentenced to execution in South Korea because they opposed the existing regimes and possibly because they had too much popular support; but they were not left-wing. In Iran the resistance against the Shah was popular and spontaneous; little of it was marxist-led. In Chile supporters of Christian Democracy are persecuted along with marxists and socialists. Working class militants and trade unionists, peasant and urban neighbourhood organisations, students, schoolchildren rebelling in Soweto, may have no particular political allegiance. Religious leaders and missionaries sometimes join the opposition and are themselves the object of repression. In Salvador Archbishop Romero was murdered for protesting against the injustices of the United States-backed government; in Brazil Archbishop Helder Camara is a noted opponent of the dictatorship; in Chile the Church has strongly protested against the persecution of the opponents of the Pinochet regime; in Colombia the priest Camilo Torres fought with the guerillas; and in Nicaragua one of the most prominent *Sandinistas* was a priest, Ernesto Cardenal.

In a number of countries, despite the repression, regimes have come to power following revolutionary struggles and wars of liberation which claim to be socialist — in Russia, Eastern Europe, China, Korea, Cuba, Vietnam, Angola, Mozambique, Guinea-Bissau, Nicaragua. We should not be uncritical of these regimes. Many of their failings are well known. These are, in part, the inevitable result of an oppressive world system. Until this system is defeated on a world scale, it is bound to limit drastically what can be achieved in any particular country. But the shortcomings and difficulties of existing post-revolutionary societies need not demoralise us: they show only that the process of building new and more just forms of social organisation is a long and uneven one. The experiences of such societies have indeed shown that there is hope that the apparently unresolvable problems of massive poverty and hunger can in fact be resolved. The problem is a political rather than a technical one; it has little to do with the overwhelming weight of population increases, an overcrowded planet, or whatever.

That this is so has been dramatically shown in the case of China, in spite of its current shift to the right. China contains nearly a quarter of the world's population; Chinese famine on a massive scale was confidently predicted before 1949. The Chinese situation can most obviously be compared with that of India. Although food production per cultivated acre in China is probably about 50 per cent higher than it is in India, food production per head is estimated to be roughly the same in both countries. Yet it is widely agreed that more or less everybody in China is adequately fed whereas in India malnutrition is chronic and starvation is not uncommon. Although inequalities in China undoubtedly persist, systematic attempts have been made to ensure that inputs are distributed fairly among communes, that the communes where land is poor are brought up to the standard of the more fertile areas and, within the communes, work and its rewards are collectively organised and there are no landlords and foreigners to appropriate the benefits. As the Brandt Report says, referring to the specific case of reforestation: 'Experience in China has shown that the combination of a strong political commitment at the top with broad public participation and shared benefits at the bottom can provide a basis for rapid reforestation.' Elsewhere the Report cautiously says:

> In [India and Bangladesh], as in most of the Third World, even in the years when overall food supplies have been adequate, this has not put an end to hunger and malnutrition. Both food and incomes have not been evenly enough distributed ... China has given food production the highest priority, and has managed — not without difficulties — to maintain adequate growth in food supplies and improve their distribution.

Yet before the revolution in 1949, the situation in China was no better than elsewhere and indeed to some observers it appeared quite desperate: William Vogt for example, in *Road to Survival*, wrote in 1948:

> China quite literally cannot feed more people ... the greatest tragedy that China could suffer, at the present time, would be a reduction in her death rate ... millions are going to die. There can be no way out ... These men and women, boys and girls, must starve as tragic sacrifices, on the twin altars of uncontrolled reproduction and uncontrolled abuse of the land and resources.

Most importantly perhaps, the experience of revolutionary struggles in the Third World has shown the power that people have to organise together to overthrow oppressive governments and economic systems, and the creative energies that can be unleashed in such struggles. Whatever may be said of the achievements or lack of achievements of existing societies that lay claim to socialism, there is little doubt that the building of new forms of society is necessary if we are to escape from the anarchy and brutalities of the current world order. As Engels wrote in a letter to Marx in 1865,

> Too little is produced ... But *why* is too little produced? Not because the limits of production ... are exhausted. No, but because the limits of production are determined not by the number of hungry bellies, but by the number of *purses* able to buy and pay.

We need societies in which what is produced is determined by need, rather than by the profit calculations of individual business people. According to marxists, socialism is a form of society in which decisions are made consciously by the people as a whole, who control democratically what is produced, how it is produced and how it is distributed, and in which the full and free development of individuals and of their capacity to control their own lives becomes possible. As Engels wrote in *Socialism: Utopian and Scientific*:

> Only under socialism will people themselves more and more consciously, make their own history — only from

that time will the social causes set in movement by them have, in the main and in a constantly growing measure, the results intended by them. It is the ascent of humanity from the kingdom of necessity to the kingdom of freedom.

Socialism or Barbarism?

In the world as in nations, economic forces left entirely to themselves tend to produce growing inequality. Within nations, public policy has to protect the weaker partners. The time has come to apply this precept to relations between nations within the world community.

Thus the Brandt Report. By 'economic forces' Brandt presumably means market forces. For 'economic forces' do not produce 'growing inequality' within, say, the social organisation of the Amazonian Indians, though capitalism's drive for expansion is quite likely to produce their total annihilation. It is only under the particular economic formation known as capitalism that economic relationships are arranged in such a way that they systematically produce a growing inequality.

Brandt says that 'within nations, public policy has to protect the weaker partners'. Again, this is presumably a reference to a particular phenomenon: the welfare state. The welfare state exists in a small part of the capitalist world, in fact mainly in Europe. It can barely be said that the 'weaker partners' are protected within the United States; some of them starve, and many of them cannot afford to go to hospital. Even in Europe, things are not that good under the welfare state and they are currently getting worse. The welfare state has not abolished inequality, exploitation and the appropriation of wealth by a few.

Inequality, as the Brandt Report of course recognises and deplores, is even worse internationally. But it is precisely this inequality, and the tribute from poor to rich it implies, that has enabled the ruling classes of Europe to 'afford' some reforms while retaining their own privileges and the wastefulness and gross irrationality of the capitalist system. In the countries that provide the tribute, capitalism is to be found in the raw.

There are other features of the capitalist world system, besides inequality, which appear to be inherent: waste, pollution, squalor, the promotion of useless consumption through advertising, and unemployment. It has also produced escalating arms production, the horrors of the nuclear bomb, weapons sales drives and wars on an unprecedented scale. In Britain, the right-wing of the Tory party is in government, racism and support for the far right are on the increase, the welfare state is being undermined, and cities are deteriorating as places for people to live in.

It therefore needs to be explained why we need capitalism at all. It is hard to believe that the US administration, ITT and others, who wished to prevent the Chilean people from, as Kissinger put it, 'irresponsibly' choosing to 'go Communist', are really anxious to secure for them more democracy and freedom, let alone better material conditions.

They must have in mind other considerations and these must ultimately have to do with the wealth which they continue to extract from dependent capitalist countries. Nothing else can really explain the regular resort by the ruling classes of the West to economic and military measures to forestall any prospects of countries 'going Communist'. In countries with pro-Western governments they may make the occasional token protest against violations of human rights. But basically they are prepared to sit by, and indeed sometimes applaud, as 'friendly' regimes massacre their opponents and starve their peoples. The explanation must be that Western capitalism remains committed to the profits it makes in the countries governed by these friendly regimes, the markets they provide for the products of its industry, the cheap raw materials and the cheap labour whose supplies they assure. At times of capitalist crisis and recession in the West, this is more than ever the case.

Marx said that humanity had two choices: barbarism or socialism. Sometimes it seems as though we are well on the way to barbarism. But there is still a choice.

Bibliography

Abdel-Malek, Anouar, *Egypt: Military Society*, New York: Random House 1968.

Adam, György, 'Multinational corporations and worldwide sourcing', in Radice, (ed.), (see below).

Alavi, Hamza, and Amir Khusro, 'Pakistan: the burden of US aid', in Rhodes, (ed.), (see below).

Allende, Salvador, Speech to the United Nations General Assembly, 4 December 1972, in Radice, (ed.), (see below).

Amin, Samir, *Accumulation on a World Scale: a Critique of the Theory of Underdevelopment*, Harvester Press 1978.

Appeldoorn, J.V. van, *Drought in Nigeria*, Centre for Social and Economic Research, Zaria, Nigeria 1978.

Arrighi, G. and J.S.Saul, *Essays on the Political Economy of Africa*, Monthly Review Press 1973.

Baran, Paul, *The Political Economy of Growth*, Penguin 1973.

Barnet, Richard J. and Ronald E.Muller, *Global Reach: the Power of the Multinational Corporation*, New York: Simon and Schuster 1974.

Bernstein, Henry, (ed.), *Underdevelopment and Development*, Penguin 1973.

Bettelheim, Charles, 'Debate with Emmanuel', *Monthly Review* June 1970.

Brandt: *North-South: a Programme for Survival. The Report of the Independent Commission on International Development Issues under the Chairmanship of Willy Brandt*, Pan 1980.

Castro, Josue de, *The Geography of Hunger*, Gollancz 1952.

Chenery, H.B. et al, *Redistribution with Growth*, World Bank/Institute of Development Studies, OUP 1974.

Cippola, Carlo M., *European Culture and European Expansion*, Penguin 1970.

Ehrenreich, Barbara, Mark Dowie and Stephen Minkin, 'The Charge: Genocide, The Accused: The US Government', in *Mother Jones*, November 1979.

Emmanuel, Arghiri, *Unequal Exchange: a Study of the Imperialism of Trade*, New Left Books 1972.

Engels, Frederick, *Socialism, Utopian and Scientific*, in K. Marx and F. Engels *Selected Works*, Lawrence and Wishart 1968.

Fanon, Franz, *The Wretched of the Earth*, Penguin 1967.

Feder, Ernest, *Strawberry Imperialism: an Enquiry into the Mechanics of Dependency in Mexican Agriculture*, Institute of Social Studies, The Hague.

Fitch, Bob and Mary Oppenheimer, *Ghana: End of an Illusion*, Monthly Review Press 1966.

Fitt, Faire and Vigier, *The World Economic Crisis: US Imperialism at Bay*, Zed Press 1980.

Frank, André Gunder, *Crisis: In the World Economy*, Heinemann Education 1980.

   - *Crisis: In the Third World*, Heinemann Education 1981.

   - *Dependent Accumulation and Underdevelopment*, Macmillan 1978.

- *Economic Genocide in Chile: Monetarist Theory versus Humanity*, Spokesman Books 1976.
- *Latin America: Underdevelopment or Revolution*, Monthly Review Press 1969.
- *Lumpenbourgeoisie: Lumpendevelopment*, Monthly Review Press 1972.
- 'North-south and east-west: Keynesian paradoxes in the Brandt report', *Third World Quarterly*, October 1980, vol II no. 4.
- 'Super-exploitation in the third world', *Human Futures*, Autumn 1979.
- 'The development of underdevelopment', in Rhodes, (ed.) (see below).
- 'Third world agriculture and agribusiness', University of East Anglia Development Studies Discussion Paper no. 31.
Free Trade Zones and Industrialisation of Asia, AMPO Special Issue 1977.
Galbraith, J.K., *Economics and the Public Purpose*, Boston: Houghton Mifflin 1973.
Galeano, Eduardo, *The Open Veins of Latin America: Five Centuries of the Pillage of a Continent*, Monthly Review Press 1973.
Genovese, *The Political Economy of Slavery*, New York: Pantheon 1965.
George, Susan, *Feeding the Few: Corporate Control of Food*, Institute for Policy Studies 1979.
- *How the Other Half Dies*, Penguin 1977.
Griffin, Keith, and Ajit Khumar Ghose, 'Growth and impoverishment in the rural areas of Asia', *World Development* vol. 7, 1979.
- *International Inequality and National Poverty*, Macmillan 1978.
- 'The roots of underdevelopment: reflections on the Chinese experience', *Modern China* vol. 4 no. 3, July 1978.
Grossman, Rachael, 'Women's place in the integrated circuit', *South-East Asia Chronicle*, no. 66, January-February 1979.
Hartman, Betsy, and James Boyce, *Needless Hunger: Voices from a Bangladesh Village* San Francisco: Institute for Food and Development Policy, 1979.
Hawkins, D.F., and M.G. Elder, *Human Fertility Control: Theory and Practise*, Butterworth 1979.
Hazlewood, Arthur, 'Colonial external finance since the war', *Review of Economic Studies*, December 1953.
Heath, Edward, 'Seizing the moment in the Caribbean', *The Times*, December 10, 1980.
- 'Why the seven must make a convincing gesture', *The Times*, 19 June 1980.
Hobsbawm, Eric, *Industry and Empire, Economic History of Britain since 1750*, Weidenfeld and Nicolson 1968.
- *The Age of Revolution 1789-1848*, Mentor 1964.
Ho Kwon Ping, article on Indonesia, *Far Eastern Economic Review* 27 April 1979.
- 'Asean is becoming a vegetable plot and fishpond for the developed world', *Far Eastern Economic Review* 11 July 1980.
- 'Thailand Inc.: an open door for the world's multinationals' *Far Eastern Economic Review* 23-29 May 1980.
Horowitz, D. 'The alliance for progress', in Rhodes, (ed.), (see below).

Huberman, Leo, *Man's Worldly Goods: the Story of the Wealth of Nations*, Monthly Review Press 1936.

Hymer, Stephen, 'The multinational corporation and the law of uneven development', in Radice, (ed.), (see below).

ILO, *Employment, Growth and Basic Needs: a One-World Problem*. Report of the Director-General of the ILO, Geneva 1977.
- *Poverty and Landlessness in Rural Asia*, Geneva 1976.

Kiernan, V.G., *The Lords of Human Kind: European Attitudes to the Outside World in the Imperial Age*, Weidenfeld and Nicolson 1969.

Kim, Phyllis, 'Saemaul agriculture: South Korean farmers prop up export-oriented economy', in AMPO, Japan-Asia Quarterly Review vol. 12 no. 1, 1980.

Lenin, V.I., *Imperialism: the Highest Stage of Capitalism*, Foreign Languages Press, Peking, 1970.

Letelier, Isabel and Michael Moffitt, *Human Rights, Economic Aid and Private Banks: the Case of Chile*, Washington: Institute for Policy Studies 1978.

Letelier, Orlando and Michael Moffitt, *The International Economic Order*, Washington: Transnational Institute 1977.

Lifschultz, Lawrence, *Bangladesh: the Unfinished Revolution*, Zed Press 1979.

Magdoff, Harry, *Imperialism: from the Colonial Age to the Present*, Monthly Review Press 1978.
- 'The American empire and the US economy', in Rhodes, (ed.) (see below).

Mandel, Ernest, *Marxist Economic Theory*, Merlin Press 1962.

Marx, Karl, *Capital*, vol. 1, Penguin 1976.
- *The Poverty of Philosophy*, Lawrence and Wishart 1974.
- and Friedrich Engels, *The Communist Manifesto*, Central Books 1971.

Medawar, Charles, *Insult or Injury: an enquiry into the marketing and advertising of British food and drug products in the third world*, Social Audit 1979.

Meillasoux, Claude, *Femmes, Greniers et Capitaux*, Paris: Maspero 1975.

Moore Lappe, Frances and Joseph Collins, *Food First*, Boston: Houghton Mifflin Company 1977.

Muckerjee, Ramkrishna, *The Rise and Fall of the British East India Company*, Monthly Review Press 1974.

Nyerere, Julius, 'No to IMF meddling', in *The International Monetary System and the New International Economic Order*, Development Dialogue 1980:2, Dag Hammarskjold Foundation, Uppsala, Sweden.

O'Connor, James, 'The meaning of economic imperialism', in Rhodes, (ed.), (see below).

Palloix, Christian, *Problèmes de la Croissance Ouverte*, Paris: Maspero 1969.

Palma, Gabriel, 'Dependency: a formal theory of underdevelopment or a methodology for the analysis of concrete situations of underdevelopment?' in *World Development* vol. 6 no. 7/8, July/August 1978.

Palme Dutt, R, *India Today*, Gollancz 1940.
-*The Crisis of Britain and British Empire*, Lawrence and Wishart 1953.
Phillips, Anne, 'The concept of "Development" ', in *Review of African Political Economy* no. 8, January-April 1977.
Radice, Hugo, (ed.), *International Firms and Modern Imperialism*, Penguin 1975.
Reno, Philip, 'Aluminium profits and Caribbean people', in Rhodes, (ed.), (see below).
Rhodes, Robert I., (ed.), *Imperialism and Underdevelopment*, Monthly Review Press 1970.
Rodney, Walter, *How Europe Underdeveloped Africa*, Bogle-L'Ouverture 1972.
Sahlins, Marshall, *Stone Age Economics*, Tavistock Publishers 1974.
Sampson, Anthony, *Sovereign State: the Secret History of ITT*, Coronet Books 1973.
Sen, Amartya, 'Ingredients of famine analysis: availability and entitlements', Oxford University and Cornell University, Working Paper no. 210, October 1979.
-'Starvation and exchange entitlements: a general approach and its application to the great Bengal famine', *Cambridge Journal of Economics* vol. 1, 33-59, 1976.
Shepherd, Andrew, 'Capitalism and hunger in northern Ghana', in Heyer, Roberts and Williams, (eds.), *Rural Development in Tropical Africa*, Macmillan 1981.
Sivanandan, A. 'Imperialism in the silicon age', in *Race and Class* vol. XXI no. 2, Autumn 1979.
Sobhan, Rehman, 'Politics of food and famine in Bangladesh', *Economic and Political Weekly*, vol. XIV no. 48, December 1979.
Tawney, R.H., *Religion and the Rise of Capitalism*, Penguin 1966.
Thompson, Don and Rodney Larsen, *Where Were You, Brother? An Account of Trade Union Imperialism*, War on Want 1978.
Traven, B., *The Rebellion of the Hanged*; *The Carreta*; *The March to the Monterria*; *The Cotton-Pickers*; etc.
Tressell, Robert, *The Ragged Trousered Philanthropist*, Panther 1967.
Vaitsos, C.V., 'Bargaining and the distribution of returns in the purchase of technology by developing countries', in Bernstein (ed.), (see below).
- 'The process of commercialisation of technology in the Andean pact', in Radice (ed.), (see above).
Vogt, Williams, *Road to Survival*, New York 1948.
Wachtel, Howard M., *The New Gnomes: Multinational Banks in the Third World*, Transnational Institute 1977.
War on Want, *The Baby Killer*, 1974.
Warren, Bill, 'Imperialism and capitalist industrialisation', *New Left Review* vol. 81, September-October 1973.
- *Imperialism: Pioneer of Capitalism*, New Left Books 1980.
Weber, Max, *The Protestant Ethic*, Allen and Unwin 1930.

Williams, Gavin, *State and Society in Nigeria,* Afrografika 1980.
 - *The Brandt Report: a Critical Introduction*, Third World First 1980.
 - 'The World Bank and the peasant problem', in Heyer, Roberts and Williams (eds.), *Rural Development in Tropical Africa*, Macmillan 1981.
Woddis, Jack, *Africa: The Roots of Revolt*, Citadel Press 1960.
World Bank, *Assault on World Poverty*, Baltimore and London: Johns Hopkins Press 1975.
 - World Development Report, 1980.
Woytinsky, W.S. and E.S.Woytinsky, *World Commerce and Governments*, Twentieth Century Fund 1955.

Sources of quotations not attributed in the text (in the order in which they occur).

John Quincy Adams is quoted in Magdoff, 'The American Empire'; Chamberlain and Rhodes in Dutt; Trevor Roper in Griffin, 'The Roots of Underdevelopment'; Cornuelle and President of GFC in Moore Lappe & Collins; Brozen in Baran; Borlaug in Moore Lappe & Collins; The AID-funded official in Ehrenreich et al; Quote on Depo-Provera in Hawkins and Elder; Dumont in George; Emperor of China in Frank, *Dependant Accumulation*; Voelker in Moore Lappe & Collins; Baxter in Weber; Calvin in Tawney; Mao in Mandel; English merchant in Hartman and Boyce; Mexican text in Galeano; *Charleston Courier* in Huberman; Cromer in Abdel-Malek; Quotes on situation in Ceylon, Egypt and India in Mandel; Watt in Moore Lappe & Collins; Nigerian farmer in Appeldorn; Merivale in Huberman; Quote on Brazilian North-East in Galeano; Keishkammahock Survey in Woddis; Chamber of Mines in Saul and Arrighi; Lugard in Phillips; Haley in Frank, 'Super-exploitation'; Black in Magdoff, 'The American Empire'; Bell in Alavi & Khusro, 'Pakistan'; Ellerman and CIA in Frank, 'Third World Agriculture'; Butz and Humphrey in Moore Lappe & Collins; Kennedy, Lens and Morse in Horowitz; US Tariff Commission in Adam; The World Bank in Ho Kwon Ping, article on Indonesia; Japanese Ministry in Sivanandan; Malaysian trade-unionist in Frank, 'Super-exploitation'; ZFIC in Frank, 'Super-exploitation'.

Development expert earnings - 21
Development and administ - 21

Develoy. and technology. 66
capital dram les p. S. d. 87